BEYOND THE UNEXPECTED CHANGES IN LATE LIFE

Practical strategies to boost social, emotional and physical engagement

DR JULIE BAJIC SMITH (PHD)

First published by Ultimate World Publishing 2025
Copyright © 2025 Dr Julie Bajic Smith

ISBN

Paperback - 978-1-923255-90-6
Ebook - 978-1-923255-91-3

Dr Julie Bajic Smith has asserted her right under the Copyright, Designs and Patents Act 1988 to be identified as the author of this work. The information in this book is based on the author's experiences and opinions. The publisher specifically disclaims responsibility for any adverse consequences, which may result from use of the information contained herein. Permission to use information has been sought by the author. Any breaches will be rectified in further editions of the book.

All rights reserved. No part of this publication may be reproduced, stored in or introduced into a retrieval system, or transmitted in any form, or by any means (electronic, mechanical, photocopying, recording or otherwise) without the prior written permission of the author. Any person who does any unauthorised act in relation to this publication may be liable to criminal prosecution and civil claims for damages. Enquiries should be made through the publisher.

Cover design: Ultimate World Publishing
Layout and typesetting: Ultimate World Publishing
Editor: Marinda Wilkinson

Ultimate World Publishing
Diamond Creek,
Victoria Australia 3089
www.writeabook.com.au

Dedication

For my family, who recognise how important my mission to improve the wellbeing of our elders is to me.

Contents

Dedication　　　　　　　　　　　　　　　　iii
Preface　　　　　　　　　　　　　　　　　　1
Introduction　　　　　　　　　　　　　　　　7

Part I: Defining the Unexpected Visitors 15
    Chapter 1: Changes in Health Status　　　　19
    Chapter 2: Changes in the Support Network　33
    Chapter 3: New Home Environment　　　　49

Part II: Boosting Emotional Engagement 65
    Chapter 4: Wellbeing in Late Life – What to Expect　69
    Chapter 5: Processing Grief and Loss in Late Life　83
    Chapter 6: Adjusting, Adapting and Additional Supports　95

Part III: Boosting Social Engagement 107
    Chapter 7: Compassionate Reconnection　　109
    Chapter 8: Stepping Out of the Comfort Zone　123
    Chapter 9: Making New Friendships　　　　135

Part IV: Boosting Physical Engagement 143

    Chapter 10: The Power of Face-to-Face Connections 145

    Chapter 11: One-on-One Wellbeing Activities 155

    Chapter 12: Group Wellbeing Activities 169

    Afterword 179

    Appendix 181

    Helpful Contacts 181

    Extra Affirmations 185

    Reference List 187

    About the Author 191

Preface

After I wrote *Beyond the Reluctant Move*, I knew that my writing journey was not over. There was more I wanted to share, to celebrate the lives of those who are no longer with us. I feel privileged to support elders through the late years of their lives, and their wisdom and insights help shape what I do.

This book, *Beyond the Unexpected Changes in Late Life: Practical Strategies to Boost Social, Emotional and Physical Engagement,* is intended for a wide range of audiences, including those not necessarily living in residential aged care. I wanted to share recent research – including my own learnings and insights – with elders living in their own homes, with relatives, or travelling in a caravan without a fixed address. The book is for those who may still be completely independent, as well as those receiving some support, and those who are receiving care at home or within residential aged care. It is also intended for caregivers, care managers, health professionals, families and volunteers. Through shared stories and insights from elders, this book will inspire you and provide easy suggestions on how to boost emotional, social and physical engagement without feeling overwhelmed. Additionally, I introduce two new research papers I contributed to (White, 2024a and White, 2024b) about the admission to residential care of individuals impacted by dementia.

In today's world, most of us are lucky to be able to make our own decisions about our lives and daily activities. We can choose how and where we live, the type of work we do, how we spend our money, time and energy, and when we need to rest and recharge. We thrive on the concept of independence and freedom, fulfilled with endless opportunities and choices. For those still in the workforce beyond 65, many can choose where they work, how much they put into their chosen vocation, whether they work part or full time, and how they spend time outside of work. Working beyond retirement age can be a personal choice and preference, balanced with other commitments such as family time, hobbies and interests outside of the workforce. The options are truly endless in terms of how one decides to live their life and spend their time and energy.

Older people who live healthy and fulfilled lives rarely seek help and support. They are far too busy and like to just 'get on with it'. Most do not look for alternative accommodation options if they can maintain living where they are and they are happy doing so. 'What is the point?' I have heard many tell me, using those exact four words. It is hard to plan for a different future and explore the what-if scenarios if we do not see any changes in our day-to-day lives. We cannot predict how our lives will unfold, and if we may indeed need more help and support.

Subtle changes in one's health and wellbeing may provide a little nudge that certain jobs need to be outsourced, such as maintaining lawns and garden beds or getting some domestic assistance with cleaning bathrooms, showers and floors. It can be difficult to acknowledge that we need help not because we are busy or disinterested, but because physically it is becoming difficult to complete the tasks ourselves. We are starting to slow down, and having those chores completed by someone else can be a better solution. Earlier in life, we are often more open to receiving help and support, such as getting an extra hand during childrearing years. However, as we age, it can become more of a battle for independence. Some may want to prove their ability by trimming hedges, or climbing ladders to clean the gutters or check on solar panels, which can result in a fall and catastrophic injuries.

Despite the small statistical representation of older Australians living in residential care – approximately 5% – the stories shared by workers, health professionals and many elders have enriched my understanding and interpretations of the impact of grief, isolation, loneliness and the power of social connection in this setting.

Most people I have met in aged care homes tell me that their roadblocks were mostly unexpected (even if it was a chronic health condition they battled for years) and most certainly unwelcome. Entering residential care was not something they ever envisioned in their lives, and they took pity on others who had to go through the process. Many elders end up in residential care suddenly, and the sudden change of environment can have a profound impact on their emotional wellbeing. The timing of one's admission to residential care is crucial. If the process is rushed or the person is already requiring significant support and lacking insight into their own skills and abilities, they may have difficulty adjusting to receiving help and support, and to their changed environment.

Even moving into a retirement village can be perceived as a negative step, associated with ageing and requiring support. Several elders I met experienced negative emotions after moving into a brand-new state-of-the-art retirement village. Despite initially perceiving the change to be positive and luxurious, it became a reality of their own ageing process. It required acceptance of being surrounded by peers or older counterparts, rather than seeing neighbourhood kids running up and down the driveway, squealing in excitement.

In recent years, many of us have experienced reduced social interactions with our neighbours and loved ones following the Covid-19 pandemic, and potentially have had less awareness of our own health and support needs. Several relatives of elders who moved into residential care shared that it was difficult to assess how their loved one with dementia was coping at home, as they had less contact than normal and were unable to assess the environment.

The impact of the Covid-19 pandemic has significantly contributed to how we live, work, travel, socialise and interact with one another. One of the big issues in our society that has been brought to light by the pandemic is loneliness and isolation across the lifespan. It is not just the elderly who feel disconnected from our society; younger generations are experiencing it too. We have learned just how important it is to check in on one another, to ask people how they are, or if we have not seen our neighbour for a while, make sure they are safe and well.

Many people are at risk of experiencing emotional changes due to the pressures of everyday life. While isolation and loneliness are experienced by people of all ages, in late life they have been identified as a predictor of functional decline and death (Perissinotto et al., 2012). For elders who may be experiencing changes in their health status and support network, it is even more important to help them stay connected and involved in their community.

This book is not about predicting the possible changes that we may have in late life. There are no specific chapters on dealing with falls, neurological and cardiovascular conditions, and so forth. No two people are alike, and our own experience will differ from another person going through the exact same challenge. This book will offer strategies on how to deal with life after we experience such unwelcome changes, exploring how we can move beyond them to continue to experience rich lives filled with many physical, social and cognitive activities that are good for us and our wellbeing. There is life after being diagnosed with dementia, there is life after having a fall, and there is life after changing one's living environment. It is important that we remember this and remind our elders that we are here for

Preface

them as they navigate through the challenges they are going through. Together we will get through this – I am going to show you how.

We live in an interesting time. The impact of the Covid-19 pandemic has heavily influenced how our elders live and interact with society. Many still have a significant fear of Covid, and this is impacting their engagement and interactions with others. There are a number of strategies we can implement to enrich the lives of our elders, to help and support them gently and mindfully through the changes they may be experiencing. Building resilience and strength will take time; it is a skill that requires energy and effort. Through the strategies offered in this book, we can reflect firsthand on how this has been achieved with many elders and how you too can help and support those in your care, whatever stage of life they are in.

I hope you enjoy reading this book and gain ideas and skills you can start to implement today.

Introduction

The world's population is ageing rapidly. Between 2015 and 2050, the proportion of the world's older adults is estimated to almost double from about 12% to 22% (World Health Organization). This is incredible growth. In absolute terms, this is an expected increase from 900 million to 2 billion people over the age of 60. This signifies the importance of supporting elders and assisting them in living not only longer but also better, which can be achieved in many instances without pharmacological intervention.

Changes form a part of our everyday life. Some changes come as a pleasant surprise and can generate positive emotions. A nice sunny day in the middle of a cold and wet winter can make us feel happy, a surprise birthday party thrown by loved ones can leave us feeling grateful, or a long-distance friend visiting can make us feel excited. These pleasant changes generally generate positive emotions and experiences. On the other hand, we can experience sudden and not-so-happy moments, unwelcome changes that disrupt our usual health status and routine and result in negative emotions. This may be a minor setback, for example, getting the dreaded flu and missing out on a family gathering or rolling an ankle and having difficulty getting around, which can leave us feeling frustrated, sad and disheartened. A wide range of experiences can shape our emotional responses to events and our views of ourselves and the world around us.

Most changes only impact our daily life for a short period before we get back into the swing of our normal routines and health status. The 'thank goodness it was nothing serious' moments may result in us making healthier choices, such as improving our exercise, nutrition and increasing safety awareness if needed. Throughout our life, we may experience bigger changes, including moving countries, losing a loved one or experiencing a sudden change in our health. Bigger changes may take a longer time to adjust to and require more resilience and strength to overcome. Sometimes, when a person was perhaps too young to remember, they may not have realised the impact of the big change they experienced earlier in life, often leaving some to wonder just how resilient they were at the time.

As we age, changes can become more challenging to accept. Older adults may find that they are addressing many challenges at the same time, and this may feel quite overwhelming. Even a seemingly small change can feel too much to handle.

What do you mean bins are now collected on Tuesdays and I have to separate my rubbish into three separate bins?

Oh no, Joan and Frank are moving away. We will no longer commute together to the volunteer centre and have lunch on Wednesdays. I will now have to go alone.

Broadly speaking, changes in late life fall into one of the following categories:

- health
- relationships

Introduction

- finance
- new environment.

These changes may be something older people experience either quickly or slowly. Sudden changes are those which occur fast and almost seemingly overnight, such as a sudden setback in one's health, losing a loved one, suddenly changing living environments, or becoming homeless and experiencing financial setbacks. Slow changes, on the other hand, are those that happen gradually over time, such as when a loved one is starting to show early signs of memory and personality changes and is eventually diagnosed with dementia, adjusting to retirement and the changes that come with fulfilling our day-to-day activities, and gradual changes in one's health, strength and endurance. Regardless of the change, and whether it is quick or slow, an individual may still find at times that it feels too much, too soon and becomes unbearable.

Why are we focusing on the ageing population?

We are living longer than ever before. The pace of population ageing is much faster than in the past. According to the World Health Organization, in 2020, the number of people aged 60 years and older outnumbered children younger than 5 years. By 2030, 1 in 6 people in the world will be aged 60 years or over.

In Australia alone, as of 30 June 2020, there were an estimated 4.2 million older Australians (aged 65 and over), with older people comprising 16% of the total Australian population (ABS 2020b). By 2066, it is projected the number of older Australians to have increased to over 10 million (ABS, 2018). We are working and living longer and retiring later. Many elders are occupied with numerous social, vocational and physical activities after turning 65, which provides a sense of fulfillment, contribution and engagement. Aged care homes often see many elders volunteering and supporting residents, and residents, in fact, sometimes respond better to encouragement from a volunteer to leave their rooms and join activities than from a staff member.

Importantly, it is becoming clear that there is no typical older person, whether living in their own homes or in residential aged care. We are all unique today, and we will continue to be unique in our later life. In today's world, some 80-year-olds have physical and mental capacities similar to many 30-year-olds. Other people may experience significant declines in their physical and mental capacities at much younger ages. The diversity seen in older age is not random. According to the World Health Organization (2023), a large part arises from people's physical and social environments and the impact of these environments on their opportunities and health behaviour. Across the world, older people are often assumed to be frail or dependent and a burden to society, which is incorrect. This is an example of an ageist attitude that can lead to discrimination, influence how policies are developed, and affect the opportunities older people have to experience healthy ageing. Today, older people are becoming more and more diverse, with different socioeconomic backgrounds, life experiences and lifestyles. These factors all influence the ageing process and affect one's health and wellbeing.

What are our best options for the future, and are we ready for the challenges?

We are slowly getting there. Our awareness of the factors associated with positive and successful ageing is growing. We will all experience different challenges as we get older, some more significant than others. We are more aware of risk factors for stroke, heart attacks and developing dementia. Dementia, in particular, is a growing concern for many people, and we are becoming more aware of things we can do to minimise the risk of developing this disease and factors we cannot change. Non-modifiable risk factors, which we cannot change, include:

- age – as you age, the risk of dementia increases
- genetics – there are a few very rare forms of dementia associated with specific genes
- family history – a family history of dementia increases your risk of developing dementia, but at this stage, it is not clear why (Dementia Australia, 2023).

Modifiable risk factors, which can be changed through lifestyle choices, have been well researched. You can reduce your risk of dementia by looking after your heart health, body health and mind health.

Does ageing bring on grief and loss?

Everyone experiences grief at some stage; it is a natural part of life. However, in late life, it becomes accumulative, meaning that we may experience more of it and far more frequently than in our younger years. Recognising the impact of grief in late life on our health and wellbeing is important, as is uncovering the root causes of it. Importantly, not all grief is associated with death and dying, and much of it still allows space for growth and acceptance despite one's age.

Older adults may grieve the past and the future. Grief about the past may include the loss of a loved one, a time when one was in good health, and grief around independence and more freedom. Grief can also be about the future that one anticipated, or it can be about anticipating the death of a loved one who may be in poor health, and neither of you will have the future that you both imagined of growing old together.

One of the strategies shared on this topic is recognising the emotional impact of grief and loss we may experience. This includes recognising if an individual may require additional emotional support and providing opportunities to debrief and access more structured support through counselling. Talk therapy can be beneficial for grief and anticipatory grief, particularly if an individual may be at an increased risk of developing long-term complications and has a limited support network.

Affirmations

An affirmation can be any positive statement that resonates with you and can be helpful at times of processing any type of loss or change. Throughout this book, affirmations will be shared at the end of each chapter to inspire and encourage the older person, regardless of the change they may be facing. Sometimes, it can be the missing statement in a conversation to let a person know that someone cares about them, that it is safe to share their feelings, and that they are still powerful and resilient despite the unwelcome changes they may be experiencing in their lives.

Affirmations may include statements such as:

- It is safe for me to explore my emotions.
- It is safe for me to seek support for my emotions.
- It is safe for me to get upset.
- It is safe for me to share my emotions with others.

What types of resources are helpful?

A renowned Australian psychiatrist, Ian Hicke, highlighted that 'tools do not fix the problem; people who use the tools solve the problem'. Recognising when and what type of tool to use is important.

Introduction

There are several tools you can find by visiting wisecare.com.au that have been prepared with you in mind:

- **5 Facts About Me Worksheet:** an easy, fast and effective exercise in getting to know the elders in your care.

- **20 Strategies For Changes in Late Life:** this exercise will help you improve conversations with those impacted by changes in late life.

- **Supporting Elderly Clients With a Reduced Family and Social Network Flowchart:** an easy-to-follow flowchart to determine an action plan to help your client based on their unique needs.

- **Free Book Chapter:** access a free chapter of my book *Beyond the Reluctant Move*, which offers a range of strategies to assist those entering residential care.

There is so much to share to help you boost the emotional, social and physical engagement of an elder. If you are an elder yourself, I want you to know, you can still make a beautiful life for yourself even if you experience an unwelcome change.

Let's get started!

Part I

Defining the Unexpected Visitors

The Guest House

This being human is a guest house.
Every morning a new arrival.

A joy, a depression, a meanness,
some momentary awareness comes
as an unexpected visitor.

Welcome and entertain them all!
Even if they're a crowd of sorrows,
who violently sweep your house
empty of its furniture,
still, treat each guest honorably.
He may be clearing you out
for some new delight.

The dark thought, the shame, the malice,
meet them at the door laughing,
and invite them in.

Be grateful for whoever comes,
because each has been sent
as a guide from beyond.

Rumi

Oh, the unexpected visitors – they can cause quite a stir. The type we do not anticipate, and particularly those who tend to linger. How we entertain them largely depends on our own resilience, experience, and views of ourselves and our world.

Defining the Unexpected Visitors

Three of the most common unexpected visitors in late life are changes in health, changes in support network and changes in living environment. In this section, we will explore each one of those changes, and in later sections, we will make suggestions on how to boost emotional, social and physical engagement despite these changes.

CHAPTER 1

Changes in Health Status

Happiness is the highest form of health.

Dalai Lama

Let's start with some hard truths. Everyone will experience some type of health change as they age – it is inevitable. However, the exact type and extent of change will vary from person to person. Ageing is not a rapid process that happens overnight and impacts us all equally once we reach a certain age. We do not suddenly wake up one morning grumbling, 'I am officially old and can no longer do anything by myself'. There is no magical number where one should feel, look and identify as being old. Someone in their 70s may be more fit and healthy than someone in their 50s. Our genes, lifestyle and habits can determine the type of ageing we may experience but cannot guarantee that we will not encounter unexpected difficulties and setbacks. In this chapter, we will examine some of the common health conditions that older adults may encounter in their late life and the impact these conditions may have on resilience and coping. This does not mean that you will experience all or any of those changes, but someone close to you might. Others may experience a range of symptoms without a formal diagnosis, which can lead to uncertainty and fear. In this book, suggestions and recommendations will be made for this population as well.

This book is not about self-diagnosis or finding the key to addressing a specific medical condition. The intention is not to be too caught up in the diagnosis part. This is a common mistake made by many in assuming that 'my loved one has dementia; they cannot do anything anymore' or 'my loved one is depressed – there is nothing that can be done to help them' or 'fractured femur – not going to walk ever again'. We are looking beyond the aspect of the health change that occurred to better understand how to support the individual in their present moment and given their current health status to help them move forward. Of course, some changes can be more sudden than others, particularly accidents. However, accidents can happen throughout our lives. Certainly, these events can cause significant physical pain and a range of emotional responses, including embarrassment, stress, anxiety and trauma. In many cases, we can heal and recover both physically and emotionally and make adaptations as necessary and move on with our lives. As CS Lewis famously said, 'You are never too old to set a new goal or to dream a new dream.'

As we approach our midlife, we may start to notice some subtle changes or niggling pain in our joints, reminding us that 'Arthur' is here – an affectionate nickname several elders from an aged care home shared when referring to rheumatoid arthritis. This can be frustrating but not overly alarming. Once we approach retirement age, we may start to experience changes in some of our senses, such as our hearing or vision. Or perhaps, our mobility and balance may be impacted, reducing our tolerance for being physically active and independent with housework and community access. For some, it may be just one change, for example, reduced hearing, that can have a profound impact on quality of life and social interactions. For others, it could be a combination of changes such as strength, endurance and agility impacting independence. Perhaps we need to say goodbye to surfing and long-distance running and embrace tai chi and aqua aerobics, or replace hiking with shorter walks around the neighbourhood. This change and adaptation can be hard for some, who may be hard on themselves about their health changes, leaving them feeling stuck and despondent without a clear indication of their prognosis or alternative activities they may be able to safely complete. The world can become a scary place when we feel out of our comfort zone.

One of the biggest fears for many is changes in cognitive functioning, including the potential diagnosis of dementia. There may be a whole range of factors impacting an individual, which could result in memory changes due to sudden medical episodes and from virtually any poorly controlled chronic disease of the brain or the body's organs. The good news is that some cognitive changes may, in fact, be reversible. Let me explain. If we experience hearing loss, we may not be able to hear information properly, let alone recall it. However, if we address our hearing loss through appropriate aids, we may be able to hear better, and feel better about ourselves and the world around us. Hallelujah! We do not have a memory problem. Other causes of cognitive changes may be due to mental health conditions, such as depression, which again, if treated properly, can see improvements in one's functioning and memory through improvement in social engagement and connection. This realisation has been huge for many who have had concerns that their memory change was irreversible.

Self-diagnosis of dementia, that is diagnosis not given by a health professional, can result in individuals becoming more withdrawn and fearful of their health and future. Addressing barriers that can be improved with technology, talk therapy, aids and appliances can make a profound change in an individual and their support network.

Good vs Bad Days

Without a doubt, we can all experience good and bad days when it comes to our health. We may have a day when we feel great, then the next day does not feel so good. It is unrealistic to expect every day to be perfect and for our health to be optimal. Some of the bad days can be particularly difficult, especially if they result in a poor night's sleep and worries about the future, leading to uncertainty and fear. For some individuals, getting support can be easier than for others, who may feel defeated and hard on themselves about receiving help, thinking it is somehow a fault on their end or something to be ashamed about. Being open to receiving practical support from family or strangers can be difficult for people of all ages. This is particularly so for some older adults, who may perceive it to be an indication of loss of independence.

Psychologically, exploring the difference between good and bad days is usually done by counting which type of day takes the lead – the good or the bad. If we feel that we have more good days than bad, that is good news. We can still participate in many types of activities and programs and be our best most days. On the other hand, if we feel we have more bad than good days, this could be a sign that we may need more help and support. In this instance, it may be worthwhile to connect with a person you trust, such as a family member, friend or your doctor, to discuss your symptoms and concerns. Early intervention is key, and the sooner an individual receives the required support, the better they may feel. Receiving psychological support can also be challenging, with many unable to safely open up about their worries and fears. Older adults respond to psychological interventions, such as Cognitive Behavioural Therapy (CBT), as well as their younger counterparts. This is particularly encouraging knowing that there are gains to be made, improvements, and new skills that can boost wellbeing and their overall outlook on life.

Physical Health Changes

Physical health changes can range from general mobility decline without a specific cause to more specific health conditions that have a formal diagnosis. Some are gradual, such as reduced mobility due to osteoporosis or arthritis impacting the joints, whereas others are sudden, such as fractures, heart attacks (which can occur at any age) or cerebral vascular accidents (CVAs, also known as strokes). Chronic health conditions, which are persistent or long-lasting, such as diabetes, chronic obstructive pulmonary disease (COPD), emphysema and Parkinson's disease, can impact individuals both physically and emotionally. For example, Parkinson's disease can result in tremors, which can affect the ability to complete tasks requiring fine motor skills, and also emotionally, with the loss of confidence and self-esteem. Similarly, CVAs can impact mobility, speech, swallowing and emotional regulation. This is just a brief overview of the types of physical health changes, and of course, there are many more that can be included.

Emotional Changes

Emotional changes range from isolation, withdrawal and social disconnection to more formal diagnoses, including anxiety, depression, adjustment disorder, bipolar affective disorders, late-onset psychosis and schizophrenia. Emotional changes can also be due to chronic mental health conditions, which can become more difficult to manage in later life, particularly in combination with changes in physical health status. It is important to note that an individual may have experienced a condition, such as depression, for a long period of time prior to their physical health change, for example, macular degeneration or CVA. Learning to tease apart which came first can take time, but it is important to know in order to avoid attributing everything to 'old age'.

Dementia and Cognitive Changes

Did you know that some elements of cognitive change are normal in old age? However, the presence of dementia is not. We will explore this in more detail, including the different stages of dementia that individuals may experience. While running wellbeing workshops over the years in retirement villages, this topic usually drew large crowds and led to lengthy discussions. Some of the most common questions included:

- What is dementia?
- What can we do to minimise the risk of experiencing it?
- How can we support those who may be impacted by this disease?

Prevention strategies were sought, and recognising early signs in oneself and their loved ones was emphasised. Strategies recommended reflected research over the last several decades, which broadly highlight the importance of looking after one's physical health, remaining socially connected and improving lifestyle factors. In most cases, recommendations from the World Health Organization (2020) for reducing the risk of cognitive decline were discussed, with the latest version of those at the time of publication listed in the table that follows.

Changes in Health Status

> 1. *Be physically active*
> 2. *Cease smoking*
> 3. *Eat a balanced diet; most preferably Mediterranean*
> 4. *Drink alcohol in moderation*
> 5. *Practise cognitive training*
> 6. *Be socially active*
> 7. *Look after one's weight*
> 8. *Manage hypertension*
> 9. *Manage diabetes*
> 10. *Manage cholesterol*
> 11. *Manage depression*
> 12. *Look after one's hearing and manage hearing loss.*
>
> World Health Organization (2020)

Cognitive changes are usually attributed to three broad types of neurological conditions:

1. Mild cognitive impairment
2. Early onset dementia (symptom onset before the age of 65)
3. Dementia

Before beginning to experience mild cognitive impairment, older adults may be in a preclinical and silent phase where they may begin to experience brain changes without measurable symptoms. Individuals may notice changes, but these changes may not be detectable on tests. This may be a stage where the patient knows that something is not okay, but the doctor does not. The patient may be afraid to bring it up with their doctor, in fear of what happens next, and often this stage can be a silent stage whereby the symptoms are not discussed, and the person's symptoms of memory change become more advanced. For individuals with a limited support network, it can become even more difficult to recognise mild cognitive impairment, as they are simply not having enough social engagement and connection where someone may be able to notice these changes.

Mild Cognitive Impairment (MCI)

Mild cognitive impairment is a condition in which people have more memory or thinking problems than other people their age. Cognitive changes may not impact activities of daily living, but they may be of concern to the individual and their family. It is possible that the individual may have one or more cognitive domains that are significantly impaired, such as their short-term memory. In this instance, the individual may repeat themselves several times without realising it, misplace household objects, forget where they parked their car in a shopping centre, or not remember when and where they noted down their next review with a doctor. Individuals experiencing mild cognitive impairment can become frustrated, short-tempered and anxious about their cognitive change, which can affect their coping skills and resilience.

Mild cognitive impairment may be an indicator of dementia but not always. It is important for elders to know this, as the thought of a dementia diagnosis can be frightening and overwhelming. There could be many causes of mild cognitive impairment, such as stress, side effects of medication, trauma, mental health conditions, recent hospitalisation or changes in environment.

Dementia

The ageing process is often negatively associated with dementia. Many assume that as people age, they become demented. This is not the case. Dementia is not a normal part of ageing; however, one's risk of developing dementia does increase with age. Dementia is a syndrome, usually of a chronic or progressive nature, in which there is deterioration across three main domains – memory, behaviour and the ability to perform everyday activities. It is estimated that 50 million people worldwide are living with dementia, with nearly 60% living in low and middle-income countries. The total number of people living with dementia is projected to increase to 82 million in 2030 and 152 million in 2050. There are significant social and economic issues in terms of the direct costs of medical, social and informal care associated with dementia. Moreover, physical, emotional and economic pressures can cause great stress to families and carers. Support is needed from the health, social, financial and legal systems for both people with dementia and their carers.

Dementia: The Umbrella

Dementia is the umbrella term for a number of neurological conditions, of which the major symptom is a global decline in brain function. The most common type of dementia is Alzheimer's disease followed by vascular dementia. Some individuals may be diagnosed with a 'mixed type' of dementia, indicating they exhibit symptoms from more than one type. Mixed dementia is much more common in older age groups, such as those over 75 years.

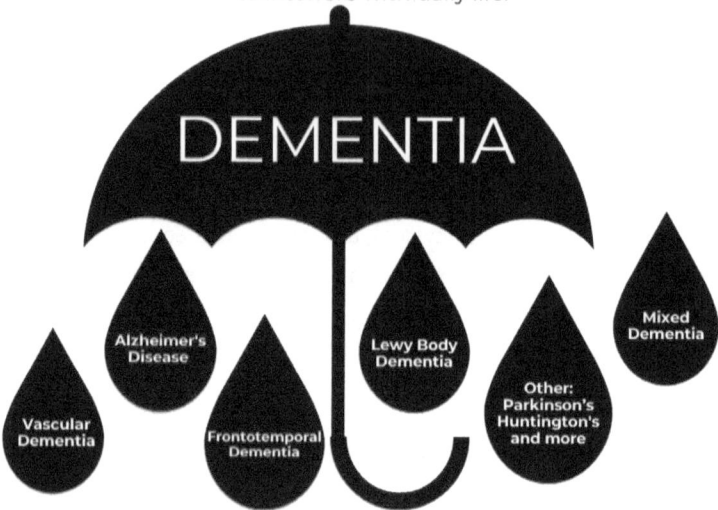

Each type of dementia has different symptoms and causes. It is important for individuals to learn more about the type of dementia that their loved ones may have in order to understand how to best support them.

Important Statistics About Dementia

- **Dementia is the second leading cause of death in Australia.** According to the Australian Institute of Health and Welfare (2022), provisional data indicates that dementia may soon become the leading cause of death.

- **Dementia is the leading cause of death for women in Australia.** (Australian Institute of Health and Welfare, 2022).

- **In 2023, it is estimated that over 400,000 Australians are living with dementia.** Without a medical breakthrough, this number is expected to rise to more than 800,000 by 2058 (Australian Institute of Health and Welfare, 2022).

- **In 2023, it is estimated that over 28,650 people have younger onset dementia,** which can affect individuals in their 30s, 40s and 50s. This number is expected to increase to more than 42,400 by 2058.

- **In 2023, more than 1.5 million people in Australia were involved in the care of someone living with dementia.** Two in three people with dementia are thought to be living in the community (Australian Institute of Health and Welfare, 2022).

- **More than two-thirds (68.1%) of aged care residents have moderate to severe cognitive impairment** (World Health Organization, 2020).

The Role of Family in Dementia Care

Family plays a crucial role in supporting individuals with dementia symptoms and diagnosis. Family members are often the first to raise concerns with health professionals and engage service providers. However, those who visit occasionally, especially during the holiday season, may not witness the daily symptoms that primary caregivers observe. This can lead to misunderstandings, gaslighting, and minimisation of the caregiver's role and experiences.

Statements like, 'I think Mum is totally fine, why are you making such a fuss?' can be unhelpful. Occasional visitors may only see the older person for a short period, during which they might have had a pleasant conversation and reminisced about the good old days. In contrast, caregivers who see the older person regularly can notice more evident changes, such as forgetting to take medication, ignoring expiry dates on dairy products, burning food and leaving the tap or gas on.

Addressing this inconsistency in perception is important, preferably without the older person present, to minimise the impact on their wellbeing. Accepting that a loved one's health has changed can be difficult and may result in grief over losing a parent, spouse or friend to dementia. This process, often referred to as the 'slow goodbye', involves witnessing changes in the person's characteristics, habits and personality right before our eyes.

In this chapter, we reviewed several types of health changes that can impact individuals aged over 65, or over 50 for those from Indigenous backgrounds. Health challenges tend to be one of the most significant setbacks an older person may experience, and it can be difficult to feel excited about a future that may be vastly different from the one they had planned. Despite these challenges, it is important to remember that a health diagnosis does not necessarily mean that life is over. Many individuals continue to lead fulfilling lives with the right support, adaptations and a positive mindset. The rest of this book will explore ways to navigate these health changes and continue to find joy and purpose in life.

AFFIRMATIONS

Despite the arrival of unexpected visitors in late life, it is helpful to remain optimistic, think the best possible thing will happen, and hope for it even if it's not likely. Here are some affirmations to share with an elder impacted by changes in their health.

1. It is safe for me to seek positive experiences with others despite changes in my health status.

2. I can still experience good days despite changes in my health status.

3. I am not defined by my health status.

4. I am so much more than my physical health.

5. Every day is a good day; some days are better than others.

6. I can still contribute to my community, family and my own decisions, despite changes in my health status.

7. I am someone who has been through a lot, and my experience and wisdom can help me overcome challenges right now.

8. My unique experience shapes who I am, and I deserve to be heard and understood.

9. I matter, and I am not giving up on myself.

10. I am loved and supported by others, and above all, I truly and deeply care about myself.

CHAPTER 2

Changes in the Support Network

Having a support network in your life and being a part of other people's support networks, means you can add their energy and their mental, emotional and physical resources to your measure of resiliency.

Teal Swan

Our need for social connection is deeply embedded in us biologically, regardless of our age, cultural background or health status. An astonishing amount of theory and research suggests that humans have evolved the need for social connection. We all crave to be connected to others, to feel secure, included and supported, which in turn boosts our resilience. Although some of us need social connection more than others, most would agree that sharing life experiences with others feels good.

More recently, we have all unexpectedly experienced the impact of isolation. The Covid-19 pandemic has tested our tolerance for being alone for prolonged periods, with self-isolation and social distancing requirements highlighting the importance of being connected to others – something we may have taken for granted in the past. Importantly, mandatory isolation has increased our awareness that some members of our community may not have a strong support network in place, resulting in prolonged and ongoing loneliness and social isolation (George et al., 2015), even when Covid-19 restrictions eased.

In this chapter, we will untangle some of the reasons for changes in support networks and the impact these changes can have on our health, wellbeing, thought processes and behaviours. Additionally, a personal reflection on the impact of social connection by a daughter whose mother lived in an aged care home will be shared.

Types of Changes

Changes in support networks can impact many aspects of one's life, including social connections, leading to isolation, social disconnection and self-neglect. In late life, maintaining social connections can be more difficult. Sometimes, it can be sudden and defining moments, such as the death of a loved one, leaving us with profound grief, loss and a sense of loneliness from not having that special person to share our life experiences with anymore. An elder recently shared:

> *'All my friends have died. Everyone you see in this wedding photo is gone, apart from me.'*

The cumulative effect of friends and loved ones passing can be overwhelming, as well as the reality of facing one's own mortality.

Other times, changes in support networks may be due to a gradual decline in physical health, impacting one's ability to maintain social interactions, particularly if the individual is no longer able to independently attend outings and access their local community. Similarly, if the person has faced a recent change in their living environment, such as transitioning from independent to supported living, establishing new friendships and connections can be challenging and feel overwhelming. Loss of confidence and self-esteem can impact how and when we interact with others, particularly for those who have experienced multiple losses.

What is Social Connectedness?

Social connectedness can be defined as the experience of belonging to a social relationship or network (Garafalo, 2013), and notably, the size of that relationship is not as important. Being socially connected is a subjective feeling of being connected to others and having strong bonds. Social connection is not about counting how many friends one has, but more about how connected they feel to those around them.

Sometimes, it could be just that one special friendship that meets an individual's social needs and leaves them feeling heard, understood and supported. This friendship may be one that was formed recently or one that has survived many decades and changes over time. For some, that special person could be a spouse, a relative or a friend. For others, it may be a small group of people who share common interests, hobbies or outlooks on life.

You don't need a friend circle.
Just one dot is enough.
Just one true friend is enough for a lifetime.
Unknown

Benefits of Social Connectedness

Being socially connected can improve our physical health and mental and emotional wellbeing. The strength of connections is based on shared experiences and empathy. When we feel connected, we are more likely to stay physically active, socially engaged and feel good about ourselves and the world around us. Healthy connections with family, friends, partners and colleagues are known to lower levels of anxiety and depression, and even raise our self-esteem. This is a catch-22 situation, as people who are experiencing a mental health condition may want to avoid connecting with others. However, connecting with others is exactly what they need the most, as an elder recently shared:

> *'I need to be around people, even though it's not easy at times. You get out of your own head that way.'*

Studies have shown that individuals who are socially connected have higher self-esteem, greater empathy for others, and are more trusting and cooperative. In other words, social connectedness generates a positive feedback loop of social, emotional and physical wellbeing. Strong social connection leads to a 50% increased chance of longevity, strengthens your immune system, helps you recover from disease faster, and may even lengthen your life (George et al., 2015). Therefore, being connected to others is good for our bodies and souls.

Longing for social connection and companionship is not uncommon, even in those with poor health. We want to be connected to others and have a sense of belonging. Sadly, many elders living alone, with family members, and even residents in aged care homes, identify as feeling isolated and lonely due to a lack of social connection. Just being surrounded by others does not reduce isolation.

Individuals living in residential care may sometimes be surrounded by as many as a hundred other residents and still not feel any connection towards others. Other times, individuals may feel and maintain a strong connection with others despite not having physical contact. The daughter of an elderly resident of an aged care home shared:

'I said my physical goodbye to Mum some years ago.'

They live in different states in Australia, and although they have not seen each other in over two years, they have daily contact over the phone. This daughter is without question the closest person to the elderly resident. She knows her elderly mother inside out and far better than anyone else, including in-person visitors. Sometimes we think about the support network as being those who are physically present, but that is not always the case. During Covid-19 restrictions in particular, people have been separated from their families, and although they may be physically apart, it does not mean that their relationship is any less significant.

Personal Reflection on Social Connection with Loved One in Residential Care

The following excerpt was shared by a daughter of an elder who lived in residential care during the Covid-19 pandemic. This was shared with permission and prepared specifically for this publication.

I recall when I began to phone Mum on a regular basis after her admission into aged care. It was at a time when the rest of the family with whom she had lived went away on a holiday. I rang her on the first night they went away as I could tell she missed everyone. So I suggested I call her every day for the duration of the holiday. I could tell from Mum's voice just how much she enjoyed this contact with me.

And so, this daily call continued even after the family returned. I felt it was important to her mental health that we have this contact. As Mum had holidayed with me every year (I live interstate), she had made friends here and knew them all very well, so we had lots of things in common to talk about. She was always keen to know how new babies were, who had gone on a trip, who had been ill. As time went on, these daily phone calls became online calls!

This form of contact was even more special as Mum could SEE me but more importantly, I could see her. I could tell and see how she was REALLY feeling. There came times when she told me she wasn't interested in her meals. So I decided to do a video call at Mum's evening mealtime. I noticed immediately how much more she enjoyed her meal when she had company. And so, her eating improved as did her mental outlook. We discussed what little jobs she would plan for the next day, such as tidying her cupboard or beginning a small knitting project.

We were able to have our daily video calls until it became obvious to me that Mum was becoming frail and not able to manage her iPad as she once could. So I reverted to the daily phone call. Mum always loved to hear from me. She would tell me everything about her day, or she would throw in a memory, or sometimes she just didn't want to talk. But when I called the following night, it was back to normal.

I have two small dogs, and Mum knew them both. Every night she'd ask about them, and during our video call time, I would show her the dogs, and every night she'd say 'goodnight' to them. She loved seeing the dogs. I felt that Mum was almost waiting for me to call. Occasionally, if I was running late, my iPad would light up, and there she'd be ... wanting to know why I hadn't called yet! I would 'walk' Mum around my garden or around my house, which was very familiar to her. She was able to watch me feed the magpies and, in the last few months, my frogs.

So as time went on, I knew how much it meant to Mum to have daily contact. And I know how much it meant to me. Our calls ranged from 3 minutes to sometimes 45 minutes – depending on her frame of mind or if I was busy. But every day, for 3 years, I called my Mum and talked to her. We discussed everything from politics to religion to gossip or more recently, Covid. Sometimes nothing in particular. She would often give me sewing or cooking tips, and I always knew that if I wanted to know how to do something, I could always ask my mum.

As time went by, I knew her body was failing her, and this frustrated her SO much. There were things she would like to do but knew it wasn't possible. So we were able to talk through that. They were difficult times. I was also able to reinforce new rules, such as using her buzzer to go to the bathroom with a nurse. Toward the end of her life, she finally got the message! We even discussed intimate topics. Mum would tell me if something was troubling her physically but early on refrained from telling the nursing staff, so I was able to relay that information to them.

My mum has gone now, and I realise just how important this daily contact was for me! Around her evening mealtime, I look at the clock, stop what I'm doing, and go to pick up the phone to call her. I miss her love and her wisdom so much. Contact with a relative in aged care is vital. It's so important for their mental health and wellbeing. It can even have an influence on their physical health. And it costs nothing, just a few minutes of your time. Time that you AND your relative will cherish.

What Happens if We Don't Have Social Connections?

Not having good social connections can be detrimental to our physical health and emotional wellbeing. One landmark study (House, Landis & Umberson, 1988) argued that:

> *'a lack of social connection is a greater detriment to health than obesity, smoking and high blood pressure.'*

This alarming statistic demonstrates the importance of having our basic needs for security, love and a sense of belonging met throughout life.

Given the importance of social interactions, it is not surprising that most psychiatric disorders involve some disruption of normal social behaviour. When we feel unwell, we may not want to reach out to other people and may prefer to spend more time alone. At the same time, psychologically, when we explore one's strengths in recovery, having a supportive network is one of the best determinants for long-term recovery.

Circles of Support

Often, when speaking with elders, we may learn about individuals who play an active role in their lives or whose role leaves a lasting impression despite limited face-to-face contact. At times, it can be difficult to determine exactly how involved some individuals are from a practical sense and the significance of some relationships that may not generate regular connection. This is where 'Circles of Support', a simple activity that allows us to review the supports in place for an individual, can help.

A Circle of Support represents a community, providing practical advice, solving problems and generally contributing positively to the person's life. Circles of Support are based on an understanding of the importance of relationships in our lives and the need for strong support networks. There are four core circles, each representing different types of relationships. To complete this activity, there are four key questions to be asked.

Step 1: Self – What can the person do to support themselves?

This is very important for those who pride themselves on their independence. List activities, including self-awareness, that the person may have. For example, recognising when experiencing loneliness, initiating contact with others, and having the confidence to join new activities with unfamiliar people.

Step 2: Family – What role does the family play in supporting the individual? In what ways does the family help?

Does the elder have a family member or a few members who play an active role in their lives through regular check-ins, assistance with appointments, social events and opportunities for emotional support?

Step 3: Friends – What role do friends play in supporting the individual? In what ways do friends help?

Does the elder have a couple of friends who are particularly helpful and supportive? Do these people play an active role in the elder's life?

Step 4: Community – What role does the community play in supporting the individual? Which members of the community are helpful?

Are there members of the community who play an important role in the life of the elder? This could include friendly neighbours, volunteer associations or members from a local church or charity.

Outside of the Circle

Lastly, it can be helpful to gently identify who may be outside of the circle. While this may seem like a delicate activity, understanding which individuals are not currently offering help and support can provide clarity on who truly forms part of the support network. This can be challenging, as we may have strong emotional attachments to individuals who no longer play an active role in our lives.

Reduced Support Network

Sadly, some individuals find themselves with a significantly reduced support network, or even no network at all, due to various circumstances. They may have always been private, grown apart from their families, or moved away and lost contact with their connections. The impact of limited support may have led to the individual moving to supported accommodation as they age, no longer able to cope with living independently without any supports in place.

Circumstances can vary greatly, and it may not be necessary to explore the root causes, as this could cause additional distress. In these situations, it is recommended to focus on the present moment and how best to support the individual in their current situation. This requires skill in identifying safe topics for reminiscence, goal setting and care planning. One effective strategy is to explore the individual's strengths. How have those strengths helped them overcome challenges in the past, and how they can use those same strengths now? By using this approach, we are more likely to engage the individual and have a positive outcome in the conversation. This will be covered in more detail later in the book.

Social Disconnection and Self-Neglect

Self-neglect is a complex matter and one that can be difficult to address if we do not know the root cause. Is the person of sound mind? Have they intentionally neglected their personal, physical, environmental and financial care? Or have they perhaps experienced a change in their cognitive functioning that can attribute to this change? Did they lose a loved one? Are they in a new environment? There are many different factors and circumstances to consider when exploring self-neglect.

Self-neglect broadly describes three subtypes: intentional self-neglect, unintentional self-neglect, and Diogenes syndrome. Let's examine each one in more detail.

Intentional (Active) Self-Neglect

Intentional self-neglect usually encompasses self-neglect across various domains, such as lifestyle, fear of institutionalisation, personality type and maintaining control. This occurs when an individual, who is of sound mind and body, chooses to live in unsafe and unsanitary conditions. They may decide not to bathe, take necessary medications, or clean and maintain their home, even though they know they should. These decisions may be an attempt to maintain control, a lifestyle choice, a personality trait, or a reaction to the fear of going to an aged care home.

Even if the person moves into residential aged care, they may still exhibit intentional self-neglect, feeling that it is the only way they can maintain a sense of control. Statements like, 'no-one is going to make me eat/drink/do anything' are common. Sadly, with intentional self-neglect, these individuals often start to experience more health complications and may require more complex care. They can be more prone to pain, sleep disturbances, psychological distress, constipation and dehydration.

Supporting someone who has already made up their mind that they do not want any help or support can be challenging. The key is to try and support the person sooner rather than later. The longer we wait, the harder it becomes to provide effective support.

Unintentional (Passive) Self-Neglect

Unintentional self-neglect can be caused by poor physical and cognitive health. Mental health conditions, such as depression or anxiety (Wolitzky-Taylor et al., 2010), can lead to confusion and make it difficult for an individual to take care of themselves or their home.

Questions like, 'What is the point? I feel down in the dumps, and no-one will visit me', or 'Is it Tuesday or Saturday? Who cares?' reflect the mindset of someone struggling with these issues. The fear of the outside world, such as concerns about Covid-19, flu or colds, can also contribute to their reluctance to leave the house. Additionally, symptoms or a diagnosis of dementia can complicate the situation further.

Statements like, 'No, I am not demented, YOU have memory problems, not me', highlight the distress and confusion that can accompany cognitive decline. Over time, their bodies may become dirty, and their homes may become cluttered and unsafe. The individual may not understand what is happening, causing them more distress, and they may not actively choose to live in such conditions. If they lack a support network, there may not be anyone to notice these changes in their ability to provide self-care.

Another example of unintentional self-neglect could be due to changes in vision. For instance, if a person has macular degeneration, glaucoma or diabetes, their ability to keep their house and body clean can become more difficult, and they may lack insight into how bad the situation has become. Discussing it can cause more angst and discomfort.

Diogenes Syndrome

Diogenes syndrome is a response to late-in-life trauma, such as the loss of a long-time spouse or caregiver. It is a very rare condition, impacting less than 1% of the population, and we simply do not know enough about it. People with this condition often show signs of severe self-neglect, social isolation and hoarding. They may live in unsanitary conditions and not be fully aware that these conditions are unsuitable. Individuals affected by this condition lack insight into the extent of their symptoms.

Regardless of the type of self-neglect a person engages in, they can still benefit from help and support to improve their wellbeing, resilience and coping strategies. This is why what you do is so important.

You do not need any specific qualifications or a particular role to help someone who may be experiencing changes in late life, especially if they start to engage in self-neglect.

In this chapter, we examined changes in support networks, different causes that could contribute to those changes, and the impact of self-neglect. We also learned about the impact of isolation and loneliness in late life on wellbeing and how the simple exercise of Circles of Support can be beneficial in identifying support for an elder. Many interventions have been developed to combat loneliness and social isolation due to changes in support networks among older people. The individuality of the experience of loneliness and isolation may cause difficulty in delivering standardised interventions. We cannot overgeneralise and say things like, 'just get out and meet people'. There is no one-size-fits-all approach to addressing loneliness or social isolation, and hence the need to tailor interventions to suit the needs of individuals, specific groups or the degree of loneliness experienced. Therefore, future research and services should aim to discern what intervention works for whom, in what particular context, and how.

AFFIRMATIONS

Experiencing changes in a support network can be tough throughout life, and even more so in late life. Here are some helpful affirmations to share with elders impacted by changes in their support network:

1. It is safe for me to make new friendships.

2. I truly and deeply accept myself.

3. I can do something today and focus on being in the present moment.

4. I have many interests and experiences that I can share with others.

5. It is not too late for me to learn something new.

6. I have many strengths that can help me overcome my challenges.

7. I can grieve the past and still enjoy today.

8. If I am lonely, it is safe for me to share that feeling with others.

9. I am allowed to have a bad day and know that tomorrow something will bring a smile to my face.

10. I am worthy of love.

CHAPTER 3

New Home Environment

*Life takes you to unexpected places.
Love brings you home.*

Melissa McClone

There is no place like home. Home is much more than the physical place we inhabit, our four walls, and the city, state and country we live in. Physical dwellings and locations can and will change for most of us throughout our lives. We may move from small towns to big cities, from small units to big houses, and from one country to another, or reverse the process and downsize into smaller homes, units, and shared living arrangements.

The feeling of being 'at home' is much more complex and has many layers, considering the context of the environment and its occupants. But what does being at home represent? For most, it means feeling beloved, cherished, protected and cared for. This promotes a state of safety and security and forms part of our identity. A home is a place where we feel safe; it is our fortress that shields us from the troubles of the outer world.

In late life, a sense of being at home can be achieved through independent living in a privately owned or rented property, living with relatives (moving into their established living arrangements), living in retirement communities with people of similar age, or living in residential care and having a deep sense of belonging in that environment. Many elders have shared a sense of relief when they return to their rooms in an aged care home after a busy outing with family members.

In this chapter, we will review various settings and changes that can be encountered across each environment due to changes in health, social structure and the impact of the Covid-19 pandemic, most prominently in residential care settings.

Unfortunately, the safety and security of being in a home environment can change suddenly, even if we stay in the same place. Changes can be brought on by political reasons such as wars, natural disasters including flooding, fires and storms, and the end of a relationship due to separation or the death of a loved one. Although most Australians are fortunate not to experience political violence and significant impacts of natural disasters on their homes, relationship breakdowns and the loss of a loved one are experienced more frequently. After the separation or death of a spouse, some may experience a loss of the sense of being at home. Suddenly, the house that was a home for several decades may no longer feel like a place of safety and protection. Some of us may already experience those emotions temporarily; if our loved one is away for a few days, we may find ourselves unable to relax in our home on our own and long for their return so that our minds and bodies can return to a relaxed state. The house may feel overwhelmingly large, empty and cold, with any external sounds triggering a frightened response. This may result in trouble with relaxation, sleep and missing the comfortable feeling of being at home.

Not everyone likes to stay put in one place. Some of us love to move, live in new homes, flip homes and move about quickly without getting too attached to our surroundings, yet still experience the sense of being at home. Others prefer the comfort of being in the same home, priding themselves on the timeline of longevity at the same residence, and even the thought of moving a suburb away can cause them significant distress. In late life, if we experience changes in our health and support networks, being in a new environment may trigger further emotional responses. As we get older, making new friends can become more difficult, particularly if our own health has been compromised. Opportunities to meet others may be limited, particularly post-retirement and if we are no longer able to access our local community independently. In my first book, *Beyond the Reluctant Move*, strategies were provided for adjusting to living in residential care. However, only a very small proportion of elders will end up in this type of setting. It is not a realistic concern for most that they will end up in this setting unless their health status and lack of support network warrant the move. People do not move into residential aged care solely because of their age.

Independent Living

Most older adults will remain living independently throughout their lives. This may be through government-subsidised rentals, private rentals or home ownership. Some may choose to downsize from bigger houses to smaller units or move closer to family or medical facilities if required in late life. The transition older people go through is an interesting one, marked by individual characteristics and preferences. There is no rule or policy on how and where elders should live. Those who live in bigger cities are used to the hustle and bustle of busy roads, crowded shopping centres and bustling cafes. On the other hand, those who live in smaller towns are equally adjusted to a quieter pace of life and the peace they find in nature and its surroundings. Even the notion of downsizing is not compulsory; if an older person has the means to manage their property well and they are happy in their environment, there is no reason for them to make any modifications or adjustments to their home environment.

Independent living offers the freedom to decide how and where they live and what activities they engage in. Being able to prepare their own meals, complete chores, and attend to their garden and pets brings joy to many. However, independent living can also be challenging for some, as it can expose them to loneliness and isolation due to social disconnection and a reduced support network. Similarly, preparing a meal for one can be challenging, attending to all household duties can feel overwhelming, and the thought of mowing a large backyard and having a dog who requires regular exercise can be daunting. As we age, activities that once brought us a sense of fulfillment can become difficult if we experience a change in our health status and support network. It could be argued that independent living is only as enjoyable as our own health and that of our loved ones allows it to be.

Older adults are not immune to many challenges that life may bring, including financial hardship and poverty. The increasing cost of living impacts pensioners, which may result in unstable accommodation arrangements for some, moving from one address to another, and can include homelessness. Homelessness is a significant issue impacting individuals of all ages, with a sharp increase seen in Australia since the early 2000s (Petersen & Parsell, 2014). The transitions that commonly precede homelessness in later life are widowhood, the death of a parent, marital breakdown or household disputes, stopping work, the loss of accommodation tied to a job, evictions for rent arrears, and the onset or increased severity of a mental illness, with some of the earlier research (Cohen & Sokolovsky, 1989; Crane, 2002) confirming trends experienced more recently (Granier & Sussman, 2022). Sadly, homelessness is not an easy obstacle to overcome (Grenier & Sussman, 2022; Wilson, 1995), and like many interventions, the sooner the individual is supported, the better the outcome for their overall health and wellbeing.

Independent living is not always marked by excellent health, wellbeing and an outstanding support network. Those who live independently, alone or with other family members, may experience health challenges, and it can be difficult to identify when they may require in-home support and care for activities of daily living. Receiving care can present its own challenges and opportunities. Challenges include accepting that activities which once could be completed alone can no longer be done independently, and opportunities include meeting new people and creating new support networks. Recently, a lady in her 70s who lives with her husband in a leafy town in Queensland, Australia, shared the impact of Parkinson's disease on her independence and social connections:

'I have changed my attitude to Parkinson's disease and am more accepting of the fact that I have it. I would not have met a few people if I didn't have the disease.'

The change of environment from independent living to supported living presents its own challenges and opportunities. It is challenging in the sense of recognising that the change is imminent due to health challenges, changes in the support network or financial difficulties. While the adjustment can be difficult to accept, it is not always a negative one. A number of elders who move from independent living to supported living have experienced improvements in their health status, nutritional intake and quality of engagement. Yes, it is possible to thrive in retirement living and even in residential aged care.

Retirement Living

Retirement living is still classified as independent living, as what a person does within their own home is entirely up to them, but outside their front door they are supported by the village community. Retirement living often, but not always, means downsizing and can suit many people for various reasons. There are different types of retirement villages, various sizes, denominations and locations. More modern retirement villages are vertical villages, as in high rise buildings, and some even look like luxury resorts with gyms, swimming pools and state of the art entertainment rooms. Retirement living reflects various budgets, interests and personal preferences and in recent years providers have spent significant funds on the design and appeal of accommodation options for a wide market, tackling the stereotypical views of ageing and preferences.

Older adults residing in retirement living represent a population of society which recognises the need for a safer living environment in later life. Many retirees report the benefits of living in a village, as it provides added opportunities for socialisation, networking (Garofalo, 2013) and connecting with like-minded people. Living in a retirement village still provides opportunities for independence and in-home support is only provided to those who are eligible for the service or willing to fund the service privately, such as engaging a cleaner or a personal cook.

Residents of retirement villages can experience health challenges like many elders living independently. However, retirement living can offer the added benefits of security and safety. For example, if an elder is experiencing a health setback the village can support them through this journey, including mild cognitive changes, surgeries and reduced mobility. At times, residents living in retirement villages may experience significant health challenges which may result in them moving into residential care. This transition is something that can be more difficult for some to accept than others.

Recently, I was involved with a government funded program to support residents of a retirement village which was facing demolition. A group of elders voluntarily joined the group, to improve coping strategies and assist with planning for their future living arrangements. For the residents of this village, many never thought they would have to move away from the site, or their neighbours, at this stage of their life. Our discussion led to reasons why they choose retirement living in the first place. Responses included security, stability, long-term solution, convenience, financial reasons, opportunities for engagement and to meet other people as well as easier access to the local community and public transport. The program delivered was a huge success, with many participants reflecting on their newly acquired skills including better coping strategies, daily mindfulness practice and opportunities to discuss their concerns in a supportive environment.

One participant joyfully reflected:

> *'Despite the stress of having to move homes, this program has helped me become more aware of surroundings … a bird singing, a tree in the garden. It increased my mindfulness and I feel better since I have done it.'*

Volunteer Chaplain's Reflections on the Closure of A Retirement Village

The retirement village mentioned is part of a large organisation operating in Australia. A dear friend and retired colleague reflected on their experience of the village closure and its impact.

In the closing stages of my career, I chose to attend Bible College. I embarked on a master's degree at Morling College and was awarded a Master of Arts in Christian Studies. Pastoral Care was a high point in my studies, thanks to our excellent lecturer, with Church History a close second. Upon graduation, I volunteered as a chaplain, just as I semi-retired from my professional career.

The early years of working as a volunteer chaplain were an awakening. Having spent 14 years as an academic, I mistakenly thought preaching was just another form of lecturing. I now cringe at those presentations and offer a heartfelt apology to those who endured my efforts laden with obscure historical and philosophical references. Pastors I have spoken to smile and nod, indicating they all did the same thing.

At that time, we ran Sunday services in four locations. All were 'Full Care' except for the retirement village, which was independent living. The retirement village became a special place for me. The units were set amongst lawns and flowerbeds, and a large hall served the social needs of the residents, including small group meeting rooms, an exercise room, and offices for a manager and a chaplain. Over time, the hall accumulated a piano and an organ, making it well-equipped for concerts and church services.

All the residents were active physically and socially. As function was lost, most moved to care establishments, maintaining the friendships they had established at the retirement village. It was an ideal place for the last years of life, with comfort, security and companionship in a pleasant setting. I remember the quiet of a Sunday afternoon, all washed in sunlight and lengthening shadows.

It was there that I learned to preach to a supportive and patient congregation. I received feedback from those who were truly friends. After a few years, I told a small group that I was going to do a refresher course on preaching, indicating that there was still much to learn. At this point, I knew I had arrived when one person said, 'you could teach them how to preach'. That was encouraging.

The years passed in a comfortable pattern of conducting services, preaching and then exchanging with my friends, the congregation. Attendance was good, averaging around 40 people, about 30% of the village population, well above the percentage that attend church services in the general population. I also shared in the social life of the village, attending fetes, birthdays and concerts. I had established Men's Groups at the care establishments, and to my delight, the village formed their own Men's Group. I was integrated into a happy place.

First, there was a whisper, then came the blow: the village was to close. A period of great uncertainty and distress for the residents followed, which was confusing and very painful for some. This was not just another stop on a life journey. They had chosen to spend the last years of their lives at the village, attracted by its refuge and peace. Meetings were held where residents were informed of their rights and the assistance that would be given to them to relocate. Uncertainty piled on uncertainty when it was learned that approval for the development was not yet complete, yet relocation was proceeding. This was finally corrected, but it was an avoidable extra burden.

My congregation began to fade away. First, individuals whose relatives acted quickly found new homes, then small groups found alternate and equivalent places at other facilities. Those without close relatives lingered, suffering the most. Paradise had been lost. Finally, we reached the point where only a handful remained. Our chaplain and I resolved to continue to the bitter end. We conducted Bible Study in the chaplain's office for the final weeks, and then there were none.

The decision to redevelop the site was perhaps a necessity in this time when aged care is in crisis and is an expensive service to operate. There is no doubt that the complex and extensive redevelopment of the site will allow the organisation to serve in the future, but we must be aware that there was a human price paid by those who chose to live their last days at the village but were denied. The blow required counselling, which was provided, but for those of advanced years, one wonders if it was necessary. Yes, there was a cost, in this case paid by a few – to fall back on a historical reference.

Robert Creelman – Volunteer Chaplain

Residential Care

Moving into residential care can be a stressful adjustment for both individuals and their families, especially for those impacted by dementia. As the disease progresses, carers often report gaps in knowledge, including how to access support (White et al., 2024a). The transition involves leaving behind a familiar home, cherished memories and a sense of independence, leading to feelings of loss, anxiety and uncertainty. Families may also experience guilt and worry about their loved one's wellbeing in a new environment.

A recent study (White et al., 2024b) highlighted the importance of timely diagnosis, support and interventions to improve the quality of life for people living with dementia and their carers, and to delay premature placement into care. However, it's important to note that the transition to residential care is not always difficult. Many elders have successfully adjusted and found it to be a positive and enriching experience, discovering a renewed sense of community and support that enhances their quality of life.

In residential aged care, elders can engage in social activities, form new friendships and participate in various programs designed to promote physical and mental wellbeing. This social interaction can be incredibly beneficial. As one resident aptly put it:

'It's about talking to people instead of sitting in this chair all day long.'

For many, the structured environment of residential care provides a sense of security and routine, which can alleviate the stress and distress associated with living alone. The availability of medical care and assistance with daily activities also ensures that their needs are met, allowing them to enjoy their twilight years with peace of mind.

Ultimately, while the transition to residential care can be challenging, it can also open doors to new experiences, relationships and a supportive community that enriches the lives of elders and their families.

Stress appears to be more related to cases where the move was unplanned, sudden and where all parties are not on the same page about the reasons for the move. Not many people visit and choose their preferred residential care provider before their health declines. A room cannot be reserved ahead, as we do not know if the person will require support in the future, be eligible for services, and if the desired facility and room choice will be available.

Many elders who moved into residential care did not plan for the move. In many instances, the sudden change in health status gave them no option to return to independent living, particularly for those who required a high level of care, had advancing dementia and limited support networks. Some even contemplated moving into retirement villages first but often talked themselves out of it. One elder who moved into an aged care home after a nasty fall shared her views:

> *'I just was not quite ready for retirement living. I had so much to live for and although I inspected a few villages, my own little unit seemed more suitable and comfortable for me. Since I was widowed in my early 40s, I have learned to be independent and did not rely on my three sons and their families. Now, I am in residential care and receiving help with personal care is difficult to accept.'*

Living in residential settings requires an adjustment period from many perspectives – health status, new routines, openness to receiving support with daily activities, connections with other residents and staff, and adjustment to the physical environment. These adjustments require time, patience and skills to tackle late-life challenges. While many elders experience improved health outcomes, including better nutrition and more social interactions, others may face additional challenges in a new environment. They may struggle to accept their surroundings, especially if they feel excluded from decision-making. This can lead to declining mental health, increased depression risk, self-neglect, and refusal of activities, food and care. Such residents can be difficult to engage, often having negative views of themselves and their environment, which can be triggering for others who are actively seeking social opportunities. These low moods can impact others trying to form friendships, as one elder shared:

'It's hard to meet people here who are not negative. We are here for a reason.'

Keeping active and socially engaged requires an ongoing effort for residents and staff. An elder shared how, despite recognising the importance of dining room meals, she often found herself waiting for long periods for others to join and for meals to be served, coining the term 'hurry, hurry and wait'. Others reported difficulties when pressing a buzzer and waiting for assistance to attend the toilet, describing it as 'humiliating and belittling'. Some bluntly stated, 'I am just here waiting for the coffin'. These views and experiences significantly influence the residents and those who work tirelessly to support them.

Connecting with family, friends and the wider community has always been a highlight for many residents. A sense of purpose and belonging generally boosts their wellbeing and often brings a smile to their faces. One resident shared how 'the best thing that happened this year' was a card from a volunteer who could no longer visit in person. The volunteer shared their activities, allowing the resident to reminisce about their own memories of the place. This thoughtful act was greatly appreciated and boosted the recipient's wellbeing: 'A miserable wet Thursday, so I must fill in time; hence writing a short note to a dear forever friend. I've walked to Newcastle Ocean Baths via Wharf Road, returned down Hunter Street, picked up the daily paper, read it, finished breakfast, made a few phone calls, and it is still only 9 am.'

Sharing experiences, wisdom and knowledge is a highlight for many elders, especially when asked about the secrets of their longevity. One elder shared three tips that helped them live to 103:

1. Do not worry, as worry destroys you.
2. Do not hate anyone – if you have hatred, you are like them.
3. Be agreeable – always say 'that's right' no matter what you think.

Covid-19 Pandemic

The Covid-19 pandemic has caused significant challenges across all areas of society, particularly in home and residential care environments. Social distancing practices have often led to confusion, distress and reduced social interactions. Many people working in aged care have been under incredible stress due to the pandemic, experiencing guilt and trauma, especially around investigations of 'who brought the virus to the aged care home'. The impact of the Covid-19 pandemic has posed significant challenges for older Australians, their families, and the aged care workforce. We will briefly review the impact of the pandemic across home and residential care environments and offer some strategies for dealing with unexpected changes in various contexts.

In home care settings, many elders missed out on service delivery due to fear of contracting the virus. Service deliveries were cancelled, leaving many workers without shifts and reducing their income. Reduced support hours resulted in a decline in the health status of elders, with reduced mobility, prolonged isolation and an increased risk of entering residential care. Media exposure has highlighted the issue of isolation in late life, which many may not have fully understood before the pandemic. Limited social interactions and activities led to inactivity and boredom, further contributing to loneliness. Imposed isolation may also result in sedentary behaviour, which is a factor in physical, psychological and social health problems (Maher & Conroy, 2017).

In residential settings, Covid-19 led to the introduction of Personal Protective Equipment (PPE), which impacted interactions with elders and increased communication difficulties. It also caused some fright, particularly in those with cognitive changes who had impaired insight into the pandemic. The pandemic has increased loneliness (41%) and anxiety (33%) in older people in residential care (Brydon et al., 2022).

Enforced isolation has had a huge impact on the mental health of vulnerable individuals, particularly those experiencing symptoms of dementia, which is common among residents of aged care homes, with at least two-thirds and probably more than 80% having dementia (Prince, 2014). Symptoms experienced by elders during Covid-19 outbreaks may include increased anxiety, agitation, loneliness and depression, significantly impacting their quality of life. The increased morbidity and mortality among residents may further impact their mental wellbeing, with fear of illness and death prevalent among them.

Processing these Unexpected Changes

The formula outlined below is helpful in recognising that adaptation to unexpected changes consists of three parts – acknowledgement, processing and adaptation. These steps are crucial in navigating the challenges that come with sudden changes, especially in the context of ageing. The impact of change on one's sense of self and identity can be profound, as sudden changes can disrupt the stability and routine that many elders rely on. Resilience, confidence and self-esteem can all take a hit, affecting overall health and wellbeing. Here are the recommended steps in tackling this important topic:

Step 1: ACKNOW- LEDGE *Acknowledge what has happened*	Name the emotions you may feel – let it all out. Communicate your frustration, articulate your pain points, and be as explicit as possible about how you feel and the emotions you may be experiencing. The more detailed the response, the better we can process what is going on and how we can move beyond it.
Step 2: PROCESS *Process the adjustment*	It is easier said than done, but after you have named everything involved in the process, the next step includes devising a plan on how you may process it. It does not simply mean 'forgive and forget'. The processing stage requires a range of different strategies and skills that one needs to come to terms with. For example, if the sudden change includes adjustment to one's own health needs, a discussion with a counsellor may help to process this loss. Similarly, if the loss is associated with the death of a loved one, grief counselling may be the best strategy. In other instances, it may be about reaching out to less formal support networks such as family members.
Step 3: ADAPT *Adapting to change.*	Adapting to change is yet another big step, which can be difficult to achieve but may not necessarily be, if Steps 1 and 2 were followed in order. It is not possible to jump between Step 1 and Step 3 without acknowledging what is involved in Step 2. Similarly, it is not possible to simply adjust without the acknowledgement, which is Step 1. Adjustment takes time, effort and a lot of patience. It can be difficult to come to terms with adjustments to one's own health needs, support network and different life. There is a lot to process, from changes to daily functioning to the future one anticipated and the reality of where they are in the given moment.

AFFIRMATIONS

Adjusting to changes in one's living environment can be challenging at any stage of life, and it can be particularly difficult in later years. Here are some supportive affirmations to offer to elders who are experiencing these changes:

1. It is safe for me to make any environment into my own sanctuary.

2. I am aware of the beauty of nature that surrounds me.

3. I am not defined by the environment I live in.

4. It is safe for me to say if I don't like something.

5. I am allowed to share my feelings with others.

6. I can feel safe in my environment.

7. I can close my eyes and focus on the music surrounding me.

8. It is important to me to share memories with others.

9. I can still learn a new skill.

10. I am loved.

Part II

Boosting Emotional Engagement

Our emotional state plays a crucial role in our holistic wellbeing and helps us navigate the challenges we may experience in life. Emotional engagement requires skills in addressing obstacles and building resilience through adversity. Older adults generally cope well in late life until they experience some type of unwelcome change. These changes can impact one's confidence, self-esteem and sense of purpose. The role of service providers who support elders after unwelcome changes then becomes that of bringers of hope, offering opportunities and places of healing, and delivering services based on relationship building.

In late life, emotional wellbeing can be impacted by a range of circumstances, from internal factors such as physical health setbacks and cognitive changes to external factors such as the loss of a loved one, reduced support network and being in a new environment. These circumstances can result in withdrawal, loneliness and disengagement but can also provide an opportunity for growth and resilience. Loneliness is a social instinct characterised by our perception of how well we are connected to others, regardless of the frequency of interactions. It is not something that can be measured objectively, making it more difficult to determine who may be experiencing loneliness and to what extent.

In this section, we will cover wellbeing in late life, common challenges experienced by elders that can impact coping skills, and strategies to improve adaptation and adjustment. There are a range of situations that may trigger an emotional response in late life, and our response can impact how well we cope with the situation and our perception of self and identity. Change is inevitable, and how we deal with challenges is largely determined by our resilience and skill set.

Alfred Adler, an Austrian medical doctor and psychotherapist, believed that all problems we have stem from interpersonal relationship problems. According to Adler, every time we enter a conflict or argue with someone, the root cause is the perception we have of ourselves in relation to the other person.

We will learn strategies to turn unwelcome change from a place of loss to an opportunity for healing, reduced loneliness and increased social engagement. These strategies will not only make an older person feel better about themselves but also improve their quality of life.

CHAPTER 4

Wellbeing in Late Life – What to Expect

You will be happy again, you will be more yourself than ever, you will understand your heart better when you heal, you will be okay.

Unknown

When we interact with elders, many are drawn to their wisdom and insights. Studies have repeatedly shown that there's a gradual improvement in mental health as people age and that many report achieving that elusive quality – happiness. Researchers have proposed several theories to explain this phenomenon, and most agree that it is due to life experience and better problem-solving abilities. In late life, many elders report having fewer arguments, fewer financial worries and overall better quality of life satisfaction. So, why are we then talking about wellbeing in late life if all seems fine?

Mental health and wellbeing are as important in older age as at any other time of life. Indeed, for many, late life is tracking well, and they are enjoying their retirement years until some type of unexpected visitor arrives at their door. It could be a health setback, a change in their support network, or being in a new environment. How an older person responds to changes in late life has a lot to do with their coping style, personality, outlook and resilience. In this chapter, we will review some of the risk factors that impact wellbeing in late life, common mental health conditions, and propose strategies to boost emotional engagement regardless of the elder's health status and living environment. We will also suggest strategies to recognise early warning signs when an elder may be at risk of developing a mental health condition.

Older people may experience life stressors common to all people, but also stressors that are more common in later life, like a significant ongoing loss in capacities and a decline in functional ability. For example, older adults may experience reduced mobility, chronic pain, frailty or other health problems, for which they require some form of long-term care. In addition, older people are more likely to experience events such as bereavement or a drop in socioeconomic status with retirement. All of these stressors can result in isolation, loneliness or psychological distress in older people, for which they may require appropriate care and support. Mental health conditions can be present for a long time without a formal diagnosis, making it more difficult for the older person to cope with day-to-day life and challenges. Undiagnosed and untreated mental health conditions can result in self-medication and substance misuse, as individuals struggle to cope with their high levels of emotional distress. Substance abuse problems among older people are often overlooked or misdiagnosed, with the older person not recognising that they may have a problem that needs to be addressed and resolved.

Wellbeing

Wellbeing is defined as 'a state of wellbeing in which every individual realises his or her own potential, can cope with the normal stresses of life, has a sense of belonging, and engages in a community where they feel valued and loved' (Centers for Disease Control and Prevention, 2016). Mental health conditions may cause considerable suffering and result in social isolation, poor quality of life and negative impacts on families and the wider community. Like everyone else, individuals in late life can also suffer from mental illnesses. Fortunately, these disorders can be diagnosed and treated successfully, which can improve a person's day-to-day function, coping and quality of life.

There are many ways to define wellbeing. For some, it can include their physical health status or their support network. Here are three broad categories that can help us review wellbeing:

- **Emotional wellbeing:** life satisfaction, happiness, cheerfulness and peacefulness

- **Psychological wellbeing:** self-acceptance, personal growth including openness to new experiences, optimism, hopefulness, purpose in life, control of one's environment, spirituality, self-direction and positive relationships

- **Social wellbeing:** social acceptance, belief in the potential of people and society as a whole, personal self-worth and usefulness to society, and a sense of community.

Risk Factors

There are several contributing factors that impact wellbeing in late life, referred to as risks, which can influence our health and wellbeing. Some of the most common risk factors in late life include declining physical health, reduced support network, diagnosis of dementia, loneliness, social isolation and financial difficulties. Not everyone will experience all of these risks; some may experience just one, while others may face multiple risks. The most significant risk factors in late life are loneliness and social isolation. If elders feel lonely and lack a support network, this can significantly impact their health, wellbeing and outlook on life.

It is unreasonable to expect everyone to be happy and always fulfilled. Feeling sad and upset is a normal part of life and something we will all experience at some stage, regardless of our age, health status or support network. However, prolonged sadness and loneliness can be significant risk factors in late life. Not having someone to share life experiences with or to lean on for support can impact coping abilities and life enjoyment. The sense of not belonging, not feeling included, understood or supported can feel overwhelming.

Loneliness is a subjective emotional state that can include feelings of disconnectedness, psychological distance, isolation or not belonging. You can live alone and not feel lonely or socially isolated, and you can feel lonely while being with other people, such as residing in an aged care home. Just being surrounded by others does not mean that your loneliness is cured. Loneliness is the absence of connection, not company. It is difficult to measure one's loneliness without checking in with them and seeking their input about their experience. Social isolation, on the other hand, is the lack of social contacts and having few people to interact with regularly. Some people may have a supportive network of family and friends but may live far away or lack the means to facilitate frequent face-to-face interactions due to mobility or travel issues, or difficulty speaking over the phone or in person due to sensory impairment. An elder shared:

> *'My beautiful daughter visits me regularly, but my hearing is terrible, and I always get upset not being able to talk to her like I used to.'*

Both loneliness and social isolation have been linked to poor wellbeing, such as feelings of hopelessness, mental health conditions like depression and even cognitive impairment. They can also impact physical health, affecting sleep, frailty, motor function and cardiovascular health, and lead to higher mortality (Leigh-Hunt et al., 2017; Santini et al., 2020). Most recognise that mental health impacts physical health and vice versa. For example, older adults with physical health conditions such as heart disease have higher rates of depression than those who are healthy. Untreated depression in an older person with heart disease can negatively affect them, as they may lack motivation to stay active, connected and engaged in activities they previously enjoyed, such as hobbies and socialisation. In some instances, there may be additional barriers and vulnerabilities faced in late life, such as poor relationships between care recipients and caregivers. This risk factor can lead to elder abuse, which includes physical, verbal, psychological, financial and sexual abuse; abandonment; neglect; and serious losses of dignity and respect. Current evidence suggests that 1 in 6 older people experience elder abuse. Elder abuse can lead not only to physical injuries but also to serious, sometimes long-lasting psychological consequences, including depression and anxiety.

Mental Health Conditions in Late Life

Mental health and wellbeing are as important in older age as at any other time of life. Older adults, those aged 60 or above, or in Indigenous communities those aged over 50, make important contributions to society as family members, volunteers and active participants in the workforce. While most have good mental health, many older adults are at risk of developing mental disorders, neurological disorders or substance use problems, as well as other health conditions such as diabetes, hearing loss and osteoarthritis.

Mental health concerns in late life are often under-identified by healthcare professionals and older people themselves. The stigma surrounding these conditions makes people reluctant to seek help and to know what type of support will be beneficial for them, such as counselling, changing lifestyle factors or medication. The Royal Australian College of General Practitioners (2021) reports that psychoactive pharmaceuticals need to be used with care in older patients, and need to be regularly reviewed. There may be multiple risk factors for mental health problems at any point in life. In Australia, approximately 43% of people aged 16–85 years have experienced a mental health disorder at some point in their life (Australian Bureau of Statistics, 2024). However, these figures drop in late life, with approximately 14% of adults aged 60 and over living with a mental disorder, with percentages significantly higher if the older person lives in residential care settings. It is estimated that in residential care, up to one in two residents show signs of depression. This alarming statistic reflects many components of wellbeing in late life and declining physical health, including the impact of physical health on mental wellbeing, the role of support networks, and the influence of the environment on one's wellbeing.

Depression

Depression can cause great suffering and lead to impaired functioning in daily life. Unipolar depression occurs in 7% of the general older population and accounts for 5.7% of Years Lived with Disability (YLDs) among those over 60 years old. Depression is both underdiagnosed and undertreated in primary care settings. Symptoms are often overlooked and untreated because they co-occur with other problems encountered by older adults. Older people with depressive symptoms have poorer functioning compared to those with chronic medical conditions such as lung disease, hypertension or diabetes. Depression also increases the perception of poor health, and the utilisation of healthcare services and costs.

Symptoms of depression fall into four broad categories:

1. **Changes in feelings:** indecisiveness, feeling overwhelmed, lacking confidence and irritability

2. **Changes in thinking styles:** negative thinking patterns, feeling hopeless and suicidal thoughts

3. **Physical symptoms:** feeling tired, changes in sleeping patterns, feeling sick and rundown, and appetite changes

4. **Behavioural changes:** poor concentration, turning to alcohol and other drugs, and not engaging in usually enjoyable activities.

Depression can often be masked by other health conditions such as Parkinson's disease or dementia. Symptoms can be attributed to mobility issues experienced due to physical health conditions or side effects of medication. This can result in depression being missed by doctors in routine consultations, particularly if they did not know the person for a long period or due to time constraints did not have an opportunity to get to know the person when they were in better health. Older people diagnosed with depression may not have had a history of depression in earlier life. Symptoms of depression can include a combination of the above categories. Older people are often more comfortable reporting pain and physical symptoms, and may talk about their 'nerves' while denying that emotionally they may not be doing well, fearing what sharing that information may mean for their current functioning and required supports.

Anxiety Disorders

Anxiety is more than feeling stressed and different from our normal reaction to everyday events. Anxiety in late life is less researched than depression, with many symptoms normalised as, 'Betty was always like that' and not recognised as a mental health condition. Anxiety can also be situation-dependent, such as when an older person is awaiting surgery or has relocated to a new environment. Usually, an individual would have a past history of anxiety disorders, experienced earlier in life prior to old age. Individuals who experience anxiety often feel very worried or anxious most of the time, find it difficult to manage their symptoms, and feel frightened by sudden feelings of intense panic and being overwhelmed.

Similarly to depression, symptoms of anxiety fall into four broad categories, as outlined below:

1. **Changes in feelings:** sudden, intense panic, feeling overwhelmed, fearful and irritable

2. **Physical symptoms:** sweating, difficulty sleeping, muscle pain, restlessness and feeling on edge

3. **Behavioural changes:** social withdrawal and avoidance, poor concentration, turning to alcohol and other drug use

4. **Changes in thinking:** constant worry, recurring and obsessive thoughts.

Having a mental health diagnosis or experiencing symptoms of a mental health condition increases the risk of self-harm. In late life, there are usually fewer warning signs or explicit cues that an older person may have self-harm ideation. Often, lethargy is attributed to frailty, intentional self-neglect, or an intent to die. There is far less history of previous attempts and a greater prevalence of depression in the context of physical illness. Signs that an older person may have suicidal ideation include hopelessness, a sudden and intense desire to give away their belongings and putting arrangements in place for their estate (Fiske & Arbore, 2001).

How About Dementia?

Dementia is a syndrome, usually of a chronic or progressive nature, characterised by deterioration in memory, thinking, behaviour and the ability to perform everyday activities. It mainly affects older people, although it is not a normal part of ageing. Dementia is a neurological rather than a mental health condition. However, those impacted by dementia can also experience depression and anxiety.

How would we assess if a person who has dementia may be experiencing depression and/or anxiety?

- **For depression,** we would consider a sustained low mood despite engaging in usually enjoyable activities, changes in sleep patterns, lack of energy, persistent negative or dark themes and agitation. We would also need to check in with family members who have known the elder prior to their diagnosis of dementia to obtain a full history of their wellbeing prior to late life, to understand if they had a past history of depression or had accessed treatments in the past.

- **For anxiety,** we would consider the persistence of agitation and physical signs such as changes in sleeping patterns, appetite and breathing patterns. A person with anxiety may experience shallow breathing, indicating that they are under stress. Simple breathing techniques can help the person return their body and mind to focus on the present moment.

Activities

The following activities are short and simple ways to check-in on elders and encourage wellbeing.

Activity: Self-Awareness Check-In

The following table outlines practical steps for elders to maintain self-awareness and mental wellbeing. These steps are designed to help manage daily activities, stay connected with others and take care of physical and emotional health. By incorporating these actions into your routine, you can better recognise and address early warning signs of stress or low mood and take proactive measures to improve overall wellbeing. Remember, small, consistent efforts can make a significant difference in how you feel and cope with life's challenges.

Self-Awareness Check-In

		Tick
1.	Take action as soon as you notice your warning signs. Don't wait until you are feeling overwhelmed.	☐
2.	Plan each day's activities the night before – check what is on the calendar and see if there is something you could join. Motivating yourself the night before can be easier to achieve and give you something to look forward to.	☐
3.	Try to get out of bed at your planned time. Avoid sleeping in or napping during the day, as this could make you feel even more lethargic.	☐
4.	Be realistic about how many tasks you can do – go easy on yourself!	☐
5.	Find someone to talk to regularly – a friend, family member, or a neighbour. You need regular SOCIAL CONTACT. Try not to avoid talking to people and isolate yourself – this makes your mood worse.	☐
6.	Get some physical exercise every day – gentle walking and activity. Keeping active and moving is good for your body and mind.	☐
7.	Try to spend 15 minutes in the sun every day. If it is cloudy or too hot, try to get close to a window. Even looking out the window can do wonders for our wellbeing.	☐
8.	Read a funny book, watch a light video, and listen to music that you enjoy. Avoid traumatic or depressing films or books.	☐
9.	Think about activities that make you feel good physically, to overcome numbing and help you stay in your body (wearing your favourite clothes, being in the sun, taking a shower, putting moisturiser on your skin).	☐
10.	Remember that low moods pass; focus on living one day at a time.	☐

Activity: Complete the Statements

Reflecting on our experiences and emotions can be a powerful way to gain insight and foster a sense of gratitude and purpose. The following incomplete sentences are designed to help you or an elder express thoughts and feelings about ageing, happiness and personal strengths. By filling in these sentences, you can create a meaningful narrative that highlights the positive aspects of life and the wisdom gained over the years. This exercise can also serve as a valuable tool for self-awareness and emotional wellbeing.

The best thing about my age is _____

My advice for anyone over 80 is _____

_____ *makes me happy.*

I am very thankful for _____

When I feel sad I _____

Successful ageing to me means _____

I really enjoy _____

I keep active by _____

Something I learned recently is _____

Looking back on my life, my three top strengths would have to be:

1. _____

2. _____

3. _____

AFFIRMATIONS

Adjusting to our wellbeing needs requires patience and self-love. Here are some compassionate affirmations to offer to elders who are experiencing emotional changes:

1. It is safe for me to share with others how I feel.

2. I can have a good laugh and not feel bad about it.

3. I can enjoy a moment of silence, with or without others.

4. It is safe for me to tell others when I feel low.

5. Getting help and support for my emotions is not a sign of weakness.

6. I am strong.

7. I matter.

8. I make a difference.

9. I deserve to be listened to without any judgement.

10. I am me.

CHAPTER 5

Processing Grief and Loss in Late Life

Grief, I've learned, is really just love. It's all about the love you want to give, but cannot. All that unspent love gathers up in the corners of your eyes, the lump in your throat, and in that hollow part of your chest. Grief is just love with no place to go.

Jamie Anderson

Working in aged care settings often leads to discussions on grief and loss in late life and different coping styles when elders are approaching death or pass away. Many of us have experienced personal grief and loss, and this topic is not always related to death.

When discussing grief, it can be challenging to recognise what is a normal part of grief and what may be a sign that someone requires additional help and support for their emotional wellbeing (Weber, 2001). If we do not know the individual well or their circumstances, it can all feel quite overwhelming and confusing.

Grief and loss in late life is a popular topic for continuing professional development and has been offered for a number of years through Wise Care. Training sessions often lead to longer debates encompassing overgeneralisation, ageism and bias. As a society, we tend to overgeneralise grief as a part of getting older along with sadness, memory problems and mobility issues – 'of course she is always sad. She is 82 years old, alone, has poor memory, and cannot get around as much'. These stereotypes, also referred to as ageism, are beliefs we may have towards an older person based on prejudice (i.e. how we feel) and discrimination (i.e. how we act towards others based on their age).

In this chapter, we will explore what grief represents in late life, helpful versus unhelpful coping strategies, personal experiences on grief by an elder bereaved in late life, and strategies he has used to help him cope. We will complete the chapter with some practical strategies and checkpoints for when we have concerns for ourselves or our loved ones.

What is Grief?

Grief is a normal part of life and the natural emotional response to the loss of someone close, such as a family member or friend. It can also occur after a serious illness, a divorce or other significant losses such as moving countries and losing support networks. It should not come as a surprise that we may all experience grief throughout our lives due to various circumstances. Grief often involves intense sadness, and sometimes feelings of shock and numbness, or even denial and anger.

According to the TEAR model of grief, we go through four stages. First, accepting the reality of the loss. Second, experiencing the pain of the loss (allowing yourself to feel and not avoid any feelings). Third, adjusting to the new environment without our loved one. Last but not least, reinvesting in a new reality. According to this model, and many others, we learn that we do not cure people from grief, but instead we support them with their new reality (Attig, 2001).

It is important to note that grief itself is not an illness, but if prolonged and unresolved, it could lead to other barriers. Everyone uses different coping strategies and processes grief in their own way. How we cope with grief is largely shaped by internal factors, such as coping skills, as well as external factors, such as our cultural background.

Factors Associated with Coping with Grief

How a person copes with grief is affected by:

- **Cultural and religious background:** Cultural and religious beliefs can significantly influence how a person experiences and copes with grief. Different cultures and religions have unique rituals, practices and perspectives on death and mourning. These can provide comfort, structure and a sense of community during the grieving process. For example, some cultures have specific mourning periods and ceremonies that help individuals process their loss, while others may emphasise the celebration of the deceased's life.

- **Coping skills:** Coping skills refer to the strategies and techniques that individuals use to manage stress and emotional pain. These skills can be developed over time and may include activities such as journalling, meditation, exercise or seeking professional counselling. Effective coping skills can help individuals navigate the intense emotions associated with grief and find healthy ways to express and process their feelings.

- **Mental health history:** A person's mental health history can impact how they cope with grief. Individuals with a history of mental health conditions, such as depression or anxiety, may find it more challenging to manage their grief. Pre-existing mental health issues can exacerbate the emotional pain of loss and may require additional support and intervention to ensure the individual's wellbeing.

- **Support systems:** Having a strong support system is crucial for coping with grief. Support systems can include family, friends, community groups and professional counsellors. These networks provide emotional support, practical assistance and a sense of connection during a difficult time. Feeling supported and understood by others can help individuals feel less isolated and more capable of navigating their grief.

- **Social and financial status:** Social and financial status can also influence how a person copes with grief. Individuals with stable social and financial resources may have better access to support services, such as therapy or support groups. Financial stability can also reduce stress related to practical concerns, such as funeral expenses or loss of income. Conversely, individuals facing financial difficulties or social isolation may experience additional challenges in coping with their grief.

Grief in Late Life

Grief and loss are often misunderstood topics, particularly in late life, where they do not exclusively represent loss associated with death and dying. In fact, they are rarely about this topic. The main difference between experiencing grief in early life versus late life is the frequency at which it may be experienced. An older person may experience the loss of a relationship through death or separation, changes in their health status, changes in their support network, and moving into a new environment. Experiencing these changes in a short period of time may leave one feeling overwhelmed. Most reactions to grief are within the normal range, but some reactions, particularly prolonged ones that continue to present at the same high intensity, may indicate that a person has other barriers that have not been detected or treated.

Understanding that emotional symptoms present during times of grief can also be symptoms of depression, complicated grief (Mayo Clinic, 2021; Miller, 2012) or other mental health conditions is critically important. This understanding can be learned through continuing professional education, so that elders can be best supported and their concerns appropriately escalated. On one hand, there is a misconception that experiencing grief indicates one has a mental health condition. On the other hand, grief and loss in late life are overgeneralised, leading to the misconception that every elder who experiences it will end up with depression. The truth is somewhere in between. An older person may develop a mental health condition, such as depression, due to unresolved grief. However, some elders may already have depression when they experience grief.

In this chapter, we will examine in more detail the process of grieving in late life and how to overcome it. Below is an excerpt of personal reflections from a 92-year-old widower, who shared his knowledge as part of his own grief journey and wished to communicate his experiences with others. He shared these entries over a period of 6 months as he was dealing with the loss of his wife.

Experience of grief throughout life

My mother died in 1963, my father in 1969 and a sister in 2021. All of which brought great grief to our family, but for me, my wife's death was a huge shock even though the doctors had told me that she was dying. I suppose I didn't want to accept it. I think I was numb for a week or so. My middle son arranged the funeral. He could have probably seen that I was in no state to make any decisions. Even now, five months after her passing, I am having problems with the interment of her ashes.

Reaction to wife's passing

I am not quite sure of my reaction when confronted with the doctors telling us that my wife was dying. I did not want to believe it, although I understood what they were saying. My wife was drifting in and out of consciousness, I did not want to say anything to her, trying to protect her from the fact. I did not want to frighten her, by telling her this was the end. I was very distraught. I only hope I did the right thing by not telling her of the doctor's diagnosis, I could not see the point as she battled to stay alive.

Even now, months on from her passing, I still go over everything hoping that I had done it all for her before she died. When she stopped breathing, I just went numb. I could not believe that she died, even though the doctors had told us that it was about to happen. I feel ashamed that I didn't shed many tears, but I did feel great grief within. She was in all my thoughts, but I did not say much about anything to anybody. I appeared to be somewhere else. I remember returning to the nursing home late about midnight and they asked how she was, all I could get out was to say she had died. They were shocked. It didn't sink into my mind and thoughts until the funeral, 8 days later, where I was a mess.

Signs beyond the grave

My wife did come back to visit me. It was on 27 October, 10 days after her funeral service. I was calling bingo for the nursing home residents at about 11 am when I got a real queer feeling that something was going on around me. It is hard to explain, it was exterior to me, but seemed to be movement of some sort. As I continued calling the bingo until the game finished, I still had the feeling but more intense. At this point, I must say, my wife was furthest from my thoughts, as I was concentrating on the bingo and trying to work out what was going on around me. I began to get a warm feeling within my body. The feeling then moved to my chest around my heart. I then got what felt like a hot flush around my heart and then in the middle of the warmth I got a hug. I knew it was my wife. There were no words spoken but with the hug I got the feeling that she was letting me know that she was alright and not to worry. The warm feeling then just faded away and my darling was gone. Some people may say that I was imagining it. Believe me it was not my imagination, it really happened. I was overcome with emotion and my love for her is even greater if that is possible. I can't guess how she managed to get to me but it was beautiful. I often used to wonder about the life here after. I don't anymore.

Keeping memories alive

I stay in touch with my wife everyday either by reading the funeral home booklet, saying hello to her photograph on my wall or listening to our music. I am always talking to her. I always say good morning and good night to her, every day. I visit the grave, my son takes me. The one thing I am sure of is that she would be happy where she is resting now, with her mother and brother. There is room there for me to join her, when my time comes.

Loneliness and grief

I do get lonely, very lonely on occasions. Outwardly, I may appear to be okay, but my wife is always in my thoughts. Nobody to talk with intimately and otherwise, nobody to kiss and cuddle. The size of my grief equals the size of my love for her.

My wife and I still made love right up to the day she died, not like we used to in our younger days. I pushed our beds together, it wasn't as comfortable as our queen size bed that we had at our home before moving into the nursing home, but it gave us the opportunity to make love, kissing, cuddling, petting and touching and sleeping together. She always slept on my left shoulder and arm. We were very much in love, and I miss her very much.

How to Support Those Impacted by Grief

Here are some self-care strategies in how to support those impacted by grief:

G — Give yourself time to process your loss, there is no instant fix.

R — Remember to be kind to yourself and look after your needs.

I — Invest your energy in things you can change.

E — Everyone's grief experience is individual; don't compare yourself to others.

F — Find someone you can talk to about your feelings, whether it's a friend, family member, or a counsellor.

As the world looks forward, the bereaved look back, cherishing the moments spent with those who have passed. For most, the health and emotional consequences of bereavement resolve in a few months, and pre-loss functioning is restored (Wordel, 2009). One of the main concerns about this widower was that he would no longer receive psychological support as he was, in fact, doing quite well with his coping and day-to-day skills. We discussed that my role as a psychologist was not to 'cure' him from his loss, but instead to reframe this to adjusting to life after his loss. For some older people, dealing with grief and loss can be overlaid with social isolation or loneliness, particularly after their partner dies. They can be left with nothing to do or no sense of purpose (Grimby, 1993).

This gentleman was implementing many self-care strategies despite his loss, including keeping physically active, maintaining regular contact with his children, engaging in art and reading, participating in activities at the aged care facility, and frequently visiting his family and staying with them for several days at a time. This is an example of the dual process model of coping with bereavement, as outlined by Stroebe & Schut (1999) whereby a bereaved person engages in loss-oriented and restoration-oriented coping to manage feelings of grief and stressors of everyday life following the loss. Bereaved individuals can also maintain the presence of an ongoing inner relationship with the deceased person (Klass, Silverman, and Nickman, 1996), and this gentleman demonstrated how he maintains a relationship with his wife who passed away.

Supporting someone who is grieving can be challenging, but understanding and compassion can make a significant difference. The following points outline essential strategies for helping individuals cope with grief (Kübler-Ross, 1997). These steps emphasise the importance of recognising grief as a natural response to loss, allowing individuals to express their emotions, and encouraging self-care and professional support. By acknowledging the unique and personal nature of grief, we can provide meaningful support and help those affected navigate their journey towards healing.

1. Recognise that grief is a response to a loss.

2. There is no 'right way' to grieve.

3. Allow individuals to experience their grief by talking to them about their feelings.

4. Acknowledging grief will help to improve coping.

5. Encourage prioritising self-care strategies.

6. Recognise that grief does not have a timeline; however, if the intensity of grief does not reduce over time, the person may benefit from speaking with a professional. Chatting with a GP may be a good starting point.

7. Support – encourage the person to seek support from family, friends, social support groups, or specific bereavement support groups.

8. Bereavement/grief counselling – early counselling after a loss can help the person explore emotions surrounding their loss and learn healthy coping skills.

AFFIRMATIONS

Compassion and grief are deeply intertwined emotions that often arise during times of loss and change. Here are some kind affirmations to offer to elders who are experiencing grief and loss:

1. It is safe for me to be sad one day and not as sad the next.

2. Just because I don't talk about something does not mean it is not on my mind.

3. I have been through a lot, and I have come out stronger as a result.

4. It is safe for me to reflect on the experiences of grief in my life.

5. I can grieve alone, but I can also grieve with others.

6. My grief does not define me; there are many parts to my journey.

7. Some days are better than others.

8. I am a spiritual being.

9. I matter, and I am loved.

10. I believe in my potential, and I am committed to my personal growth and development.

CHAPTER 6

Adjusting, Adapting and Additional Supports

We cannot direct the wind, but we can adjust the sails.

Dolly Parton

Our reactions to events are influenced by our values, perspectives and strengths. As a result, two individuals in the same situation may respond differently, and that's completely normal. There are no set rules for how we should react to life's events. Some situations may bring joy, while others may lead to frustration, anger or sadness. In Chapters 4 and 5, we explored the emotional wellbeing aspects of late life, focusing on grief and loss, which significantly influence the changes individuals face in their twilight years. This information has helped us distinguish between what is a normal part of ageing and what indicates that someone may need additional support. In this chapter, we will examine how to adjust and adapt, facilitate additional help and support, and identify the starting points for providing such assistance.

As we grow older, navigating changes and adjustments can become more challenging due to the frequency and nature of losses we experience. Older adults may face health changes, shifts in their support network and the possibility of moving to a new environment. This complexity makes it more difficult to determine when an older person should seek professional help versus when issues might resolve on their own. Although the terms 'adjust' and 'adapt' are often used interchangeably, they describe different processes, and it's important to understand their distinctions. 'Adjust' typically refers to changes that happen relatively quickly and may be reversible or temporary, addressing specific needs or issues. For example, older adults might need to adjust to the rubbish being emptied on Tuesday instead of Friday or a change in a service provider over the summer break. On the other hand, 'adapt' often signifies a more gradual or long-term process of transforming behaviours, systems or strategies to suit a new context or overcome challenges. This might involve long-term changes, such as adapting to a new environment, to life after a loss or to changes in health status.

Activity: How Am I Feeling Today?

Understanding and expressing emotions can be a powerful tool for improving mental wellbeing, especially for elders who may be experiencing various changes and challenges in their lives. The following activity, 'How Am I Feeling Today?', is designed to help elders articulate their feelings and thoughts. By completing these sentences, they can reflect on their relationships, strengths and sources of pride and acceptance. This activity not only provides valuable insights into their emotional state but also fosters a sense of self-awareness and connection. Encouraging elders to engage in such reflective exercises can help them feel more understood and supported, ultimately contributing to their overall wellbeing.

By helping an elder complete the following sentences, we can gain a better understanding of them and their thoughts.

My family is ....
I am loved by ....
People compliment me about ....
I am good at ....
I am proud of myself because ....
I have accepted that ....
I feel good when ....
Today, I will ....

Mobility and Sensory Aids

Mobility and sensory aids can be incredibly beneficial when used appropriately and in a timely manner. For instance, hearing aids can significantly enhance engagement for those with hearing difficulties, often without others even noticing their use. More visible aids, such as walking sticks or frames, can assist individuals in mobilising after a health setback. These aids may require more time to get accustomed to, especially if the older person is also experiencing cognitive changes. Gentle reminders, prompts or physical encouragement can help alleviate any anxiety or uncertainty they may have about using these aids more frequently.

Conversely, some older adults may refuse to use mobility aids due to fear of drawing attention to themselves or concerns about the risks to their wellbeing. This behaviour, known as maladaptive avoidance, is more common in older individuals (Mohlman et al., 2011) than in younger ones. Below is a list of what maladaptive behaviours may look like. You may recognise some of these behaviours in someone you know. At times, these behaviours may not be as pronounced and may come across as incidental excuses. Over time, however, it may become more apparent that the older person is self-sabotaging engagement within their environment and local community.

In late life, some of the common maladaptive behaviours related to mobility and sensory aids may include:

- avoiding seeking help for fear of becoming a burden or losing autonomy

- refusing to use aids like canes, walkers or hearing aids due to fear of appearing old, strange or weak

- avoiding exercise or activities due to excessive fear of falling

- avoiding social events due to hearing loss or other forms of embarrassment.

Maladaptive behaviours prevent adaptation to new or challenging circumstances. For instance, using a walking stick, frame or wheelchair can make an older person feel self-conscious and anxious. They may become overly self-aware and fearful of how others will perceive them. This may lead them to reject the equipment designed to provide them with freedom and opportunities to engage with their environment.

It's crucial to address these concerns early, offering gentle support and allowing time for the older person to process what the equipment represents to them. Gentle reminders and encouragement can often lead to better outcomes.

Maladaptive behaviours can extend beyond mobility aids and sensory impairments. Other examples include:

- unnecessarily avoiding driving due to fear of crashing, getting lost or not being able to see or react appropriately

- avoiding interactions with adult children due to differing political or other beliefs, and fear of offending, insulting or starting an argument

- avoiding purchasing needed items for fear of going broke

- avoiding discarding used or expired items for fear of needing them in the future

- avoiding intellectual activities like classes or reading groups due to fear of appearing stupid

- excessive checking of blood pressure or other health indicators, financial records or the wellbeing of family members (e.g. multiple calls per day)

- over-involvement in activities as a form of distraction or an effort to control worry, such as cleaning or being overly intrusive or overprotective with adult children.

Reflection from an Elder

Below is an excerpt written by a lady seeking psychological support due to changes in her health status associated with Parkinson's disease. She reflects on her experience of receiving a diagnosis and the journey she undertook, emphasising the importance of kindness towards herself, self-reflection and being open to receiving support.

This is to summarise my discussion with you. I was telling you about my change of attitude towards my Parkinson's disease. The change is that I now try to look forward and not back. I don't feel so desperate about it most of the time as I used to.

It has not been easy to accept the changes not only to my life due to my diagnosis, but also very hard to see the effects it has on the life of my husband. He has had to take over the running of our household as well as being my personal carer. He is 78, and he has painful arthritic knees. Prior to this and my diagnosis, we both enjoyed good health and had a full and satisfying life together for over 50 years.

On the positive side, I came to realise that I have experienced good outcomes as well. I have met a lot of very nice people, and I have regular contact with younger people. I really enjoy this contact because although I am 74, I don't feel old yet in myself. Having younger people regularly to interact with is a benefit for me.

I have two gorgeous Burmese cats, and they both sleep on my bed every night. One of them is amazing. He senses that he needs to back up to me so that I can stroke him. He must realise I cannot pick him up anymore, and I need him to help me if he wants me to be smoochy with him. It is amazing how animals sense these things. I really enjoy the cats' company, and I think they add to my positivism.

I remind myself to have faith, think big and leave room for miracles.

Seeking Additional Support

Some individuals may require more support than we can provide. Signs that an elderly person might need additional assistance include persistently low mood, yearning for the deceased, difficulty engaging in daily activities and changes in eating and sleeping habits.

Discussing these issues with an elder can be uncomfortable, and we might be unsure how to approach the topic of additional support. We may also struggle to find available service providers and facilitate their engagement, especially if there are costs involved or if the booking process is complex. Recommending outreach numbers and services can be daunting, knowing that the client might be reluctant to call a stranger to discuss their feelings, particularly if they have a hearing impairment.

'I don't think I will ever get over Ivy,' an elder once shared during a consultation. Recognising his pain from losing his beloved wife, I reframed his therapy goals from 'overcoming grief' to 'adjusting to life after Ivy's death'. I explained to Ron that our goal was not for him to overcome the loss of his wife but to learn strategies and coping skills to improve his quality of life and health. Despite missing his wife, he remained active with his art, exercise, family outings and activities at the facility. He had moved past the initial shock and disbelief of her passing, and as his psychologist, I assured him that I would continue to visit. I feared he thought that if he improved, he would no longer see me. We discussed the importance of maintenance and regular check-ins to monitor his long-term adjustment, with shorter, less frequent sessions. I also encouraged him to write down his thoughts and experiences between sessions to remind him of the progress he was making every day.

Steps to Discussing Additional Support

1. Clearly identify and mention the symptoms you have observed.

2. Emphasise that help is available, and that people genuinely care.

3. Research service providers and, if possible, accompany the elder to visit their GP.

4. Share relevant information with the healthcare professional.

Today, we have more open conversations about mental health, particularly for those experiencing late-onset depression without a prior history of mental illness. Recognising that an older person may need emotional support involves observing patterns of behaviour, such as increased isolation, worry, changes in eating and sleep patterns, and feelings of hopelessness. Mental health conditions should be diagnosed by a GP or qualified mental health professional. It's important to avoid using labels and making diagnoses unless qualified to do so, and to be mindful of how we convey the need for psychological services.

Support for mental health in late life may include counselling, antidepressants and lifestyle changes. The best outcomes often result from a combination of these approaches. For those at risk of developing mental health conditions, monitoring and support with social engagement, pleasant events and exercise are crucial. Lifestyle factors, such as healthy sleeping patterns, nutritious foods and regular exercise, are vital for mental health.

Preventative strategies to boost resilience and improve coping mechanisms include exercise, social interactions, pet therapy, community engagement, and arts and crafts. Treatment options for mental health conditions usually require a team approach, including psycho-education, cognitive-behavioural therapy and other therapeutic interventions. Rebates for psychological services are available through government subsidised schemes and private health insurance.

Australian-Specific Advice

Non-GP based services, like the Swinburne Wellbeing Clinic for Older Adults, provide support via phone or video calls. These services are especially valuable for those who may have difficulty accessing in-person appointments due to mobility issues, transportation challenges or geographical distance. The Swinburne Wellbeing Clinic offers a range of psychological services tailored to the needs of older adults, including counselling, mental health assessments and support for caregivers. By utilising technology, they ensure that older adults receive the care they need in a convenient and accessible manner.

In urgent situations, providers such as Lifeline can be invaluable for immediate assistance. You can reach them at 13 11 14. Did you know that every 30 seconds, someone in Australia contacts Lifeline for help? Lifeline offers 24/7 crisis support and suicide prevention services, providing a lifeline to those in distress. Their trained volunteers and counsellors offer compassionate listening, practical advice and referrals to other support services.

For grief and bereavement support, the Australian Centre for Grief and Bereavement (ACGB) offers a variety of services for aged care residents, home care recipients, their families, friends, community workers, residential aged care staff and external organisations associated with aged care. The ACGB provides individual and group counselling, support groups, educational resources and training programs. Their services are designed to help individuals navigate the complex emotions associated with grief and loss, offering a safe space to share experiences and receive support.

Additionally, there are other non-GP based services available to support older adults:

- **Beyond Blue:** Offers support for anxiety, depression and suicide prevention. They provide phone and online counselling, as well as resources and information to help individuals manage their mental health.

- **Head to Health:** A digital mental health gateway that connects people to free or low-cost phone and online mental health services and resources.

- **Carer Gateway:** Provides practical information and resources to support carers, including counselling, respite care and financial support.

- **My Aged Care:** A government service that helps older Australians access aged care services, including home care packages, residential care and respite care.

By utilising these services, older adults and their caregivers can access the support they need to maintain their mental and emotional wellbeing. It's important to remember that seeking help is a sign of strength, and there are many resources available to provide assistance and support.

AFFIRMATIONS

Seeking additional help and support is a sign of strength, not weakness. Here are some gentle affirmations to offer to elders who may require additional assistance:

1. I feel safe seeking extra support when I'm feeling down.

2. Asking for help shows my strength, not weakness.

3. My voice deserves to be heard.

4. Sharing my story helps me understand myself better.

5. I possess great strength.

6. I have many strengths to offer others.

7. I am surrounded by love and support.

8. I welcome the wisdom others share with me.

9. I am not afraid to express my feelings when I'm down.

10. I feel safe speaking up.

Part III
Boosting Social Engagement

Humans are naturally social beings. The Covid-19 pandemic has significantly impacted our social interactions, leaving many feeling isolated and disconnected. In this section, we delve into the journey of re-engaging with others as we navigate the post-pandemic world. We will explore practical steps to step out of our comfort zones after experiencing unwelcome changes and disruptions. Additionally, we will discuss strategies for forming new friendships and connections in later life, emphasising the importance of social bonds for our overall wellbeing. Whether you're looking for suggestions on how to help elders to reconnect with old friends or make new ones, this section offers valuable insights and tips to help elders rebuild and strengthen their social network.

CHAPTER 7

Compassionate Reconnection

It's not too late to develop new friendships or reconnect with people.

Morrie Schwartz

The Covid-19 pandemic has left an indelible mark on society, affecting people of all ages. However, the elderly faced particularly severe consequences. The pandemic led to significant social disconnection, with isolation becoming a deadly adversary for many elders, severely impacting their wellbeing (Nair et al., 2023). In residential care settings, the environment and scrutiny intensified

(Tierney, Doherty & Elliott, 2022), further exacerbating feelings of loneliness and helplessness for elders (Brydon et al., 2022) and stress and burnout in the workforce (Makhado et al., 2024). The forced isolation to protect elders' health meant they were cut off from their usual support networks, leading to a devastating decline in their overall wellbeing. Facility management faced intense scrutiny as they struggled to balance safety with the need for social interaction (Brydon et al., 2022; Makhado et al., 2024).

The lessons learned during this time emphasise the importance of maintaining social connections, even in challenging circumstances. The pandemic highlighted the critical need to rebuild these connections and foster new friendships as we move forward. Social interaction is not just a luxury but a necessity for the mental and emotional wellbeing of the elderly, regardless if they live independently or in supported accommodation. The isolation experienced during the pandemic has shown that without regular social engagement, the overall health of elders can decline rapidly. Therefore, it is crucial to create environments that encourage and facilitate social interactions, even in the face of potential health risks. This involves rethinking the design and management of aged care homes to ensure that safety measures do not come at the expense of social connectivity.

This chapter aims to illuminate the importance of empathy in understanding the emotional states of older individuals. It seeks to establish whether an older person is flourishing or languishing and to adapt empathy styles to best suit their circumstances. Empathy is a powerful tool in addressing the emotional needs of the elderly, helping to alleviate feelings of loneliness and helplessness. By tailoring empathetic approaches to the unique situations of each individual, caregivers, families and health professionals can provide more effective support and improve the overall quality of life for elders. This approach underscores the necessity of a compassionate and flexible mindset in caregiving, ensuring that the emotional and social needs of the elderly are met alongside their physical health requirements.

Quick Test: Is the Older Person Languishing or Flourishing?

Determining whether an older person is languishing or flourishing involves assessing their overall wellbeing and quality of life. Languishing refers to a state where an individual feels stuck, unmotivated and disconnected, often experiencing a lack of purpose and joy. In contrast, flourishing is characterised by a sense of vitality, engagement and fulfillment. To gauge this, consider factors such as the older person's physical health, emotional state, social connections and sense of purpose.

Here are some questions to consider asking:

Are they actively participating in activities they enjoy?

Do they have meaningful relationships and a support system?

Are they able to manage their health and maintain a positive outlook on life?

When assessing an older person's ability to engage with their environment, it's important to recognise their current emotional wellbeing status. This doesn't always require a full mental health assessment; instead, reflective questions and open discussions can help determine if the person is languishing (not making progress) or flourishing (doing well) and how to support them in their current status with our own skill set; escalating appropriately if support from other service providers is required and working effectively as a team in supporting an individual and their needs.

Identifying Languishing

Definition: Failing to make progress or be successful in their current life stage.

Common signs of languishing:

- not functioning at their full capacity for their age
- diminished motivation
- every day feels the same
- less intense emotions such as joy, hope, laughter and contentment
- disrupted focus.

Languishing is not a mental health condition but can predict future poor mental health, including burnout, depression and PTSD. If languishing days outnumber flourishing days, additional support may be needed. Revisit Chapter 6 for appropriate supports and resources. Remember, compare the elder to others of similar age, not to their younger selves.

Identifying Flourishing

Definition: Living up to their full potential in their current life stage.

Common signs of flourishing:

- growing and developing successfully for their age and life stage

- setting and achieving personal goals

- high energy and drive appropriate for their age

- motivation for the future.

Positive ageing involves ongoing self-development and a positive outlook on life. An elder who is flourishing will have more good days than bad, engage well with their environment, and be an active member of their community and support network. While it's unrealistic to expect a good day every day, general trends and patterns can indicate overall wellbeing.

Empathy with Elders: The When and Why

Empathy is vital when interacting with everyone, especially those who have experienced changes in their health status. It involves understanding and sharing the feelings of others, which can significantly enhance the quality of interactions and support provided. For individuals facing health challenges, empathy helps in acknowledging their struggles, validating their emotions and offering comfort. It fosters a sense of connection and trust, making them feel heard and understood. Empathy also encourages patience and compassion, which are essential in providing effective care and support. By being empathetic, we can better address their needs, alleviate their anxieties and contribute to their overall wellbeing.

Let's explore some of the benefits of empathy.

- **Assists in building rapport:** Empathy helps establish trust and understanding, making it easier to form connections and meaningful relationships with elders

- **Encourages cooperation:** When elders feel understood and supported, they are more likely to cooperate with care plans. They know that their care team genuinely wants to improve their wellbeing.

- **Lead to better health:** Empathetic interactions lead to better health outcomes, as elders feel more motivated and engaged in their care. They feel seen, heard and understood.

- **Increase satisfaction:** Elders who feel heard and valued are more satisfied with the care they receive.

- **More effective communication:** Empathy enhances communication, ensuring that elders' needs and concerns are accurately addressed.

Defining Empathy

Many of us consider ourselves empathetic, but defining the term and distinguishing it from sympathy can be challenging. It's important to differentiate between empathy and sympathy, as they are often mistakenly seen as the same. Sympathy comes from the Greek words 'sym', meaning 'together', and 'pathos', meaning 'feelings' or 'emotions'. Sympathy involves sharing another person's feelings and experiencing their emotions alongside them. In 1909, British cognitive psychologist Edward Titchener defined empathy as 'feeling into' the emotional state of another person. Empathy is the ability to understand and share another person's feelings by putting oneself in their shoes and experiencing their emotions, thoughts and perspectives. Unlike sympathy, which is simply feeling pity or sorrow for someone else's misfortune, empathy requires a deeper connection, where one genuinely feels and comprehends what the other person is going through. Empathy allows us to see the world through someone else's eyes, with 'perspective-taking' being central to the concept. As we age, we often become more empathetic, gaining a deeper understanding of others' experiences and emotions. This emotional resonance fosters compassion, kindness and supportive interactions, making it a crucial element in building meaningful relationships and providing effective care and support.

Key Points:

- **Empathy:** Defined by Titchener as 'feeling into' another's emotional state, involves perspective-taking and understanding others' experiences.

- **Ageing and empathy:** As we grow older, our capacity for empathy often increases, allowing us to connect more deeply with others.

- **Sympathy:** Derived from Greek, it means sharing the feelings of another person, experiencing their emotions together.

Understanding these distinctions helps us better navigate our interactions and relationships, fostering deeper connections and support for those around us.

Let's explore each component of the acronym 'EMPATHY' to understand how they contribute to empathetic interactions.

E - Eye contact: Making eye contact is a fundamental aspect of empathy. It shows that you are fully present and engaged in the conversation. Eye contact helps build trust and connection, allowing the other person to feel seen and heard.

M - Muscles of facial expression: Our facial expressions convey a wide range of emotions. By being aware of and mirroring the other person's facial expressions, we can show that we understand and share their feelings. This non-verbal communication reinforces the emotional connection.

P - Posture: Your body language speaks volumes. Adopting an open and attentive posture demonstrates that you are receptive and interested in what the other person is saying. Leaning slightly forward, uncrossing your arms and maintaining a relaxed stance can all signal empathy.

A - Affect: Affect refers to the emotional tone that accompanies your words and actions. Displaying appropriate affect, such as a warm smile or a concerned expression, helps convey your genuine emotional response to the other person's situation.

T - Tone of voice: The way you speak can greatly impact how your message is received. Using a gentle, calm and compassionate tone of voice can help soothe and comfort the other person, making them feel understood and supported.

H - Hearing the whole person: Active listening is crucial for empathy. This means fully focusing on the other person, without interrupting or making assumptions. It involves listening to both their words and the emotions behind them, ensuring that you understand their perspective.

Y - Your response: Your response should reflect your understanding and empathy. This can include validating their feelings, offering support and providing reassurance. It's important to respond in a way that shows you genuinely care about their wellbeing.

By incorporating these elements into your interactions, you can create a more empathetic and supportive environment, fostering deeper connections and better outcomes for those you are supporting.

Three Key Types of Empathy

Empathy plays a crucial role in understanding and supporting others, and it can be categorised into three key types.

1. Cognitive empathy is the ability to understand how someone thinks and to see things from their perspective, recognising and comprehending their thoughts and viewpoints.

2. Emotional empathy involves feeling the emotions of others as they experience them, sharing in their emotional state and truly feeling what they are going through.

3. Compassionate empathy goes a step further by encompassing a genuine concern for the wellbeing of others and a desire to help them. It combines understanding and feeling with a proactive approach to support and care.

By recognising and practising these types of empathy, we can better connect with and support those around us. Let's delve deeper into each subcategory of empathy to understand what it entails and when we might put it into practice.

Cognitive Empathy

- **Approaching from a logical angle or perspective-taking:** This involves understanding how the other person feels and what they might be thinking.

- **Knowing the other person's thoughts and feelings:** It's crucial to avoid making assumptions about what the elder may be experiencing. Ignoring or blocking out their deeper emotions can lead to misunderstandings.

To practise cognitive empathy, ask questions, see things from the other person's perspective, feel with their heart, and listen through their ears.

Emotional Empathy

- **Feeling into the other person:** You experience their emotions almost as if they were your own, making their feelings contagious.

- **Mirror neurons:** Researchers believe that these brain cells respond equally when we perform an action and when we witness someone else perform the same action. For example, you might feel an increased heart rate while watching a game of football as your favourite team strives to win.

Emotional empathy is excellent for building close relationships, but it can be overwhelming and exhausting if you don't learn to switch it off when necessary.

Compassionate Empathy

- **Understanding and feeling:** With compassionate empathy, we not only grasp a person's predicament and share their feelings, but we are also spontaneously willing to help if needed.

- **Key ingredients:** This type of empathy involves intellect, emotion and action.

- **Holistic approach:** Compassionate empathy takes into account the entire person, considering all aspects of their situation and wellbeing.

This type of empathy is the ideal we should all aim to practice, as it strikes a perfect balance between cognitive and emotional empathy. By combining understanding with genuine emotional connection, we can offer the most effective and compassionate support to others.

Which Empathy to Use?

- Gauge the situation and trust both your thoughts and your heart to determine the appropriate type of empathy.

- If you are a professional carer, you may find yourself using compassionate empathy most frequently.

- Cognitive empathy can be particularly helpful for motivating elders, especially those experiencing emotional changes.

- Emotional empathy is useful for building rapport, but it's important to learn how to switch it off to avoid burnout.

Take Home Message

Staying connected is essential for our emotional wellbeing and overall quality of life. To achieve this, it's important to maintain regular contact with friends and loved ones, build a strong support system, keep physically active and practise self-care strategies. Achieving this can be more difficult if an older person is languishing instead of flourishing. Escalation of concerns can assist in supporting older individuals to re-establish their personal goals and improve their quality of life.

Using empathetic approaches is important, as is understanding different types of empathy and when to apply each type. At times, we may need to apply more than one type of empathy. Additionally, maintaining hobbies and interests, enjoying music and art, and interacting with pets can further enhance our sense of connection and happiness. Implementing these strategies can lead to a more fulfilling and balanced life.

AFFIRMATIONS

Forming new or re-establishing old connections can boost our wellbeing and self-esteem. Here are some helpful affirmations to support elders in the process:

1. It is safe for me to reconnect with others.

2. It is safe for me to make new friendships.

3. I am a good listener and a storyteller.

4. I care about others.

5. I am a spiritual being.

6. I enjoy connecting with others.

7. I have so much to offer to the world.

8. Today, I am connecting with my support network and people who matter to me.

9. I am a social creature and connected with my circle.

10. It is safe for me to be around others and in the company of others, it is good for me and my health.

CHAPTER 8

Stepping Out of the Comfort Zone

Dare to learn, to be different, to set your goals, to move out of your comfort zone, to be persistent.

Anonymous

Transitioning from a regular routine to discovering new activities and connections can be an exciting and rewarding experience, especially for new retirees as they explore novel social opportunities post-working life. This period offers opportunities for growth, new experiences and deeper connections with partners, particularly if they navigate life transitions together. Naturally, we all differ as we step out of our comfort zones. Changes in routine can evoke excitement in some and fear and anxiety in others, leading to questions about the reasons behind the change and one's own ability to cope with it. Much of how we approach this transition is based on our values, beliefs and health status.

In this chapter, we explore the benefits of stepping outside the comfort zone, the challenges that may arise, and practical steps to help elders boost their social engagement and embrace new experiences. By understanding these dynamics, we can better support elders in making the most of this transformative period in their lives.

Many of us recognise that change is inevitable. It brings the potential for positive transformation and new adventures, along with some adjustments that may require time and skills to master. While transitioning from a usual routine to new experiences can be exciting, it also has its downsides. This period may bring frustration, anger and resentment towards others, such as partners or other family members, as well as one's own difficulties with acceptance and adjustment to life transitions. The uncertainty and unfamiliarity of new situations can lead to stress and anxiety, making it challenging to adapt, for example, adjusting to moving from a home environment to a retirement village or supported living. Additionally, the loss of a familiar routine can create a sense of instability and discomfort.

These emotional struggles can strain relationships and impact overall wellbeing. It's important to acknowledge these challenges and seek support to navigate through them effectively, rather than just assuming that someone 'will just have to get used to it'. By addressing these issues openly and empathetically, we can help individuals manage their emotions and foster a smoother transition. This approach not only supports the individual but also strengthens relationships and promotes a healthier, more positive adjustment to new life circumstances.

Benefits of Keeping Social

Staying active and socially engaged provides numerous benefits that enhance overall wellbeing and quality of life. In later life, the advantages of social interactions include:

1. **Mental health:** Regular social interactions can help reduce feelings of loneliness and isolation, which are common among older adults. Engaging with others can boost mood, reduce stress and lower the risk of depression and anxiety.

2. **Cognitive function:** Social activities stimulate the brain, helping to maintain cognitive function and potentially delay the onset of cognitive decline. Conversations, games and group activities challenge the mind and keep it active.

3. **Physical health:** Socialising often involves physical activities, such as walking to a neighbour's house, participating in group exercises or attending community events. These activities can improve physical health, increase mobility and reduce the risk of chronic diseases.

4. **Emotional support:** Building relationships with neighbours and peers creates a network that can provide emotional support during difficult times. Sharing experiences and feelings with others can foster a sense of understanding and companionship.

5. **Sense of purpose:** Participating in local events, joining clubs or volunteering can give individuals a sense of purpose and fulfillment. Contributing to the community and helping others can enhance self-esteem and provide a sense of accomplishment.

6. **Safety and security:** Knowing and interacting with neighbours can enhance a sense of safety and security. Neighbours can look out for each other, offer assistance when needed, and provide a sense of community vigilance.

7. **Learning and growth:** Social interactions expose individuals to new ideas, perspectives and experiences. Engaging with others can lead to personal growth, learning new skills and staying informed about local happenings.

8. **Enjoyment and fun:** Socialising brings joy and fun into daily life. Whether it's sharing a laugh with a friend, attending a community event, or participating in a hobby group, these activities add enjoyment and enrich life.

It is important to recognise that elders living independently may isolate themselves due to fear of the outside world, influenced by both internal and external factors. Internally, stress and anxiety may prevent socialisation, with the perception that stepping outside of home is too frightening, particularly if one's physical health has been compromised. In such instances, smaller or shorter outings may be more realistic and appropriate. Externally, the inability to navigate uneven terrain may be a realistic concern, as well as the risk of being in close contact with others who may have a respiratory illness, such as a common cold, flu, Covid-19 or other infections that could be transmitted through airborne contact.

Keeping Social in Residential Settings

Socialising in an aged care home offers numerous benefits that contribute to the overall wellbeing of residents. Many new friendships are formed through casual interactions in common areas, by joining new activities and participating in various events. These social interactions can significantly improve mental and emotional health by reducing feelings of loneliness and isolation, which are common in residential care settings. Regular interaction with peers boosts mood, provides emotional support and creates a sense of belonging.

- Participating in group activities, games and conversations stimulates cognitive function, helping to maintain mental sharpness and potentially slow down cognitive decline. These interactions encourage residents to think critically and stay mentally active.
- Social activities often involve physical movement, promoting physical health, improving mobility and reducing the risk of chronic conditions.
- Forming connections with other residents fosters a sense of community and support, providing comfort, companionship and a sense of security.
- Engaging in social activities gives residents a sense of purpose and fulfillment, enhancing self-esteem and providing a sense of accomplishment.

It's essential to create an inclusive environment where all elders, regardless of their cognitive abilities, feel valued and supported. In an aged care setting, encouraging interactions between residents with and without dementia can break down barriers and foster understanding, combating feelings of isolation and promoting a sense of unity. Socialising brings joy and fun into daily life, with activities like music sessions, arts and crafts, and themed parties providing entertainment and enjoyment. Regular social interactions help residents build emotional resilience, allowing them to share their feelings, seek advice and receive encouragement during challenging times. By promoting social engagement and creating an inclusive environment, aged care homes can enhance the quality of life for their residents, ensuring they feel connected, valued and supported.

These are the heartfelt words of a resident who, due to isolation and the inability to handwrite notes, found solace in using a borrowed laptop to express her thoughts on the topic of stepping outside her comfort zone for the purpose of this publication:

> *'Life is very good, and I'm trying to enjoy every aspect of it. When I feel frustrated, I find that lying in bed with music playing lifts me above most of my problems. But, what I enjoy most is speaking with other residents, as it keeps my spirits up and hopefully helps them understand themselves and the world around us.'*

In residential care, joining the dining room, participating in bus trips and activities, and mixing with other residents can be both rewarding and challenging. These activities offer opportunities for social interaction and engagement, which are essential for mental and emotional health. However, there can be difficulties, particularly when there is a perception that other residents impacted by physical or cognitive changes are worse off than others, or if an individual perceives themselves and their abilities to be superior to others. This perception can create barriers to forming meaningful connections and may lead to feelings of isolation for all parties.

Understanding, acceptance and connectivity are crucial for our emotional wellbeing as we all long to be accepted, loved and supported. By promoting empathy and understanding, we encourage a sense of community and belonging. This approach not only enhances the quality of life for elders but also creates a more harmonious and supportive living environment.

Margaret, an exceptionally smart lady with reduced mobility due to a stroke, exemplifies this. Overcome with tears upon admission to a residential aged care home, she found solace in reading and connecting with a small circle of friends. 'Margaret is someone you would be proud to have met in your lifetime,' shared Carol, another resident. It was through small conversations and moments that Margaret connected with Carol, and they formed a friendship despite their health challenges and the inability of either of them to mobilise independently.

Cognitive Behavioural Model

In today's world, many of us are familiar with the concept of cognitive behavioural therapy (CBT), a widely used form of talk therapy that focuses on thoughts, feelings and behaviours. This simple yet effective approach helps us understand the fears individuals may experience around certain events. The benefit of CBT is that it clarifies problems and provides solutions, making it accessible to anyone with a little practice.

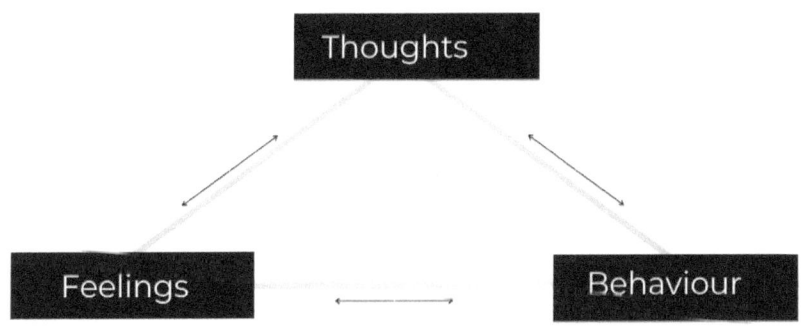

Basics of Cognitive Behavioural Therapy

Thoughts: Thoughts are the ways we make sense of situations. They can be verbal (words, sentences, explicit ideas) or non-verbal (mental images). Thoughts are the running commentary we hear in our minds throughout our lives.

Feelings: In this context, feelings refer to the physiological changes that occur as a result of emotions. For example, anger may cause our face to flush, while anxiety can make our heart pound and muscles tense. Feelings are the physical manifestations of emotions.

Behaviours: Behaviours are the actions we take or avoid. For instance, we might avoid a speaking engagement due to anxiety or seek out such opportunities if we feel confident.

In a nutshell, a situation unfolds, and our thoughts about it generate feelings, leading to behaviours that influence the situation positively or negatively. This cyclical process highlights the interconnectedness of thoughts, emotions, behaviours and their impact on ongoing situations.

Impact of Recent Events

The pandemic has caused increased stress, worry and anxiety. It is important to acknowledge these emotions, as they may feel sudden and intense. When our bodies perceive a threat, we enter a state of 'fight or flight,' an automatic physiological reaction to perceived stress or danger. During this state, our thoughts can race, we may feel dizzy or lightheaded, our breathing and heart rate can increase, and we may feel overwhelmed and unable to cope. This response impacts both our behavioural and cognitive systems.

Behavioural system: The main behaviours associated with fear and anxiety are to fight or flee. These urges can manifest as agitation or a desire to escape, often expressed through pacing, foot tapping or being short with people.

Cognitive system: The fight/flight response shifts our attention to our surroundings to search for potential threats. This heightened awareness can lead to increased vigilance about social distancing, handwashing and other activities that minimise infection risk.

Once the immediate danger has passed, the body begins to return to a more relaxed state. Heart rate and breathing slow, body temperature lowers, and muscles relax. However, residual effects of the fight/flight response may linger, leaving the individual feeling 'keyed up' for some time.

Five Strategies to Improve Coping

1. **Speak with someone you trust:** Talking through your worries with a family member, colleague, friend or counsellor can help reduce them.
2. **Visualise worries washing away:** At the end of the day, imagine your worries washing away in the shower. Take deep breaths and repeat, 'This too shall pass.'
3. **Take time out:** If emotions build up, take a short break. Even brief moments of alone time can improve endurance, wellbeing and resilience.
4. **Watch something funny:** Switch off by watching something funny, like a short YouTube video or a comedy show, to release endorphins and feel-good emotions.
5. **Maintain a journal:** Keep track of the strategies that work for you. A journal or mental notes can help you identify effective coping mechanisms and build resilience.

By understanding and applying these principles, we can better manage stress and improve our overall wellbeing.

Fact or Opinion

Understanding the distinction between facts and opinions is crucial for both mental wellbeing and effective support of older adults. Facts are objective statements that can be verified and proven, such as 'the sky is blue', while opinions are subjective beliefs or perspectives that can vary from person to person, like 'the weather is beautiful'. Despite this knowledge, our brains sometimes struggle to distinguish between the two, and harmful opinions, such as 'I'm a bad person', can be mistakenly treated as facts. This can lead to negative thinking, stress and other issues.

When supporting older adults, it is important to base decisions and advice on factual information to ensure their safety, health and wellbeing. However, acknowledging and respecting their opinions is equally important, as it validates their feelings and experiences, fostering a sense of autonomy and dignity. By balancing factual information with empathy and respect for individual opinions, caregivers can create a supportive and trusting environment that enhances the overall quality of life for older adults. With practice, distinguishing between facts and opinions can become easier, leading to better mental health and more effective caregiving.

Fact or Opinion

Let's take a look at the statements below and see if you can identify which are facts and which are opinions.

- [ ] The average life expectancy in Australia is around 83 years.
- [ ] I am a good person.
- [ ] Regular physical activity can help reduce the risk of chronic diseases.
- [ ] Gardening is the best hobby for older adults.
- [ ] My hair looks bad.
- [ ] No-one will ever like me.
- [ ] I'm not as smart as the rest of my peers.
- [ ] Social interactions can improve mental health and reduce feelings of loneliness.
- [ ] My friend is angry at me. I know this because they were frowning.
- [ ] The food in this aged care home is delicious.
- [ ] Living in a retirement village is more enjoyable than staying at home.
- [ ] I should always be nice.

AFFIRMATIONS

Stepping outside the comfort zone can be thrilling and anxiety provoking. Here are some helpful affirmations to support elders in the process:

1. It is safe for me to seek new friendships.

2. It is safe for me to make new connections.

3. Even if I feel afraid, I can take a step to learn something new.

4. It is not too late for me to start a new hobby.

5. I am open to new experiences and the joy they bring.

6. I trust myself to handle new challenges with grace.

7. Every day is an opportunity to create new memories.

8. I am deserving of love and support from those around me.

9. My past does not define my future; I can always start anew.

10. Embracing change can lead to unexpected happiness and fulfillment.

CHAPTER 9

Making New Friendships

It is always good to make new friends.

José Feliciano

Friendships offer numerous benefits that can significantly enhance our overall wellbeing, especially in late life. Some of these benefits include reduced stress and anxiety, improved mental health, enhanced physical health, a stronger support system, increased happiness, and better cognitive functioning. As we get older, many of us find it more difficult to make new friends, particularly those who share similar life experiences and outlooks on life. We may not have enough opportunities to meet like-minded people and spend quality time together. This challenge is compounded, particularly in late life, by the inevitable loss of many long-time friends. An elder recently shared:

> *'I have my little book of phone numbers that my wife and I used. Pages after pages of names and numbers of people who have now passed away.'*

Sometimes the cumulative effect of losing multiple friends can make the process of acquiring new friends even more difficult. Changes in health status, physical environment and support networks can also impact friendships in late life, resulting in isolation and withdrawal, but also presenting opportunities to form new friendships. As José Feliciano said, 'It is always good to make new friends.' In this chapter, we will show you how.

Late Life Friendships

It goes without saying, having friendships in late life is highly beneficial for our physical health and wellbeing. Friendships can improve our sense of identity, enhance physical health, decrease the risk of dementia and increase longevity. Making a friendship can truly save our lives, as face-to-face interactions help us combat many of the challenges that can arise in late life when we start to internalise our problems and worries and become detached from others.

Meeting another person in similar circumstances can reduce the void and increase a sense of understanding and acceptance. It is not uncommon for older adults to make new friendships through various avenues such as volunteer opportunities, religious gatherings, social outings and changes in living circumstances, including moving to retirement villages or residential aged care. Friendships have also been formed in hospital wards, rehabilitation centres and shared room facilities. Visiting many aged care homes over the years it became evident how quickly bonds were formed with residents whose rooms were close to one another, and in particular those in shared room environments. Even at times when one party had a higher level of support needs than the other, their understanding, support and connection was strong.

Let's now explore some of the benefits that friendships can bring in late life.

- Friendships can help you experience better mental health. This is shown through an improved sense of belonging, connection and reduced isolation. If we feel heard and valued, our self-esteem and identity are enhanced as well as our outlook on life.

- Friendships can decrease the risk of dementia. Having regular connections and engagement can reduce the risk of cognitive impairment, and keep our working memory active and sharp. We are more likely to know the difference between Wednesday and Sunday, how we spend each day and which days we socialise.

- Friendships can improve physical health. We are more likely to be keeping active and kept on our toes, spending time together with our friends and making new memories.

- Friendships can increase longevity and foster a stronger sense of purpose. If we share a life experience with someone, we feel less isolated and lonely. Having a friend, especially a peer, can boost our morale and outlook on life, particularly if we are experiencing health challenges.

Here are some further research studies which highlight the benefits of keeping friendships in late life.

According to a study published by the *Journal of Neurology, Neurosurgery and Psychology* feelings of loneliness in seniors increased their risk of dementia by more than 60% (Holwerda, Deeg, Beekman et al., 2014).

Older adults who reported feeling lonely had a 45% increase in risk of death, along with a 59% higher risk of mental and physical decline, according to another study (Perissinotto, Stijacic, Cenzer & Covisnky, 2012)

Isolated seniors experience abuse and are victims of scams at higher rates than seniors with friends and support around them, according to Hafemeister (2003)

The National Institute on Aging (2024) says socially active adults have lower levels of an inflammatory factor associated with several age-related conditions, including Alzheimer's disease, cardiovascular disease, osteoporosis and rheumatoid arthritis, along with some forms of cancer.

How Can We Build New Friendships?

Where shall one go to meet new friends? How can we support our older loved one to make new connections? The opportunities are endless! Building new friendships through common interests can be especially beneficial for elders, helping to combat loneliness and isolation. By following the below steps, elders can build new friendships based on common interests, creating a supportive and connected social network that enhances their overall wellbeing.

Here are some steps tailored to help elders forge new connections:

1. **Identify your interests:** Reflect on hobbies and activities you enjoy or have enjoyed in the past. Whether it's gardening, knitting, playing cards or attending cultural events, knowing your interests will help you find like-minded individuals.

2. **Join local clubs or groups:** Look for senior centres, community centres or local organisations that offer activities and classes for elders. Joining these groups will provide opportunities to meet people who share your passions.

3. **Attend social events:** Participate in social gatherings, meetups or events specifically designed for elders. These events are great places to meet new people and start conversations.

4. **Volunteer:** Volunteering for causes you care about can help you meet like-minded individuals. It's a great way to bond over shared values and make meaningful connections while giving back to the community.

5. **Be a good listener:** Show genuine interest in others' stories and experiences. Listening actively and empathetically can help you build rapport and deepen your connections.

6. **Start conversations:** Don't hesitate to initiate dialogue with new people. Ask questions about their interests and share your own experiences. This can help you find common ground and build a connection.

7. **Frequent local spots:** Become a regular at a local cafe, park or community centre. Over time, you'll start to recognise familiar faces and have the chance to strike up conversations.

8. **Use technology wisely:** Join online groups or forums related to your interests. Many communities offer virtual events and activities for elders. While prioritising safety, you can connect with people who share your passions and arrange to meet in person.

9. **Be approachable:** Smile and maintain open body language. Being approachable can make it easier for others to start conversations with you.

10. **Stay in touch:** Once you've made a connection, make an effort to stay in touch. Regularly check in with new friends and plan activities together to strengthen your bond.

Supporting a Loved One to Make Friendships

Everyone can make friends throughout the lifespan and it is likely that someone else is going through what we are experiencing, shares common values, interests and views on life. If one is willing to make friends and connect with another person, chances are they will make a friend. It can become more difficult to make friendships if we remain socially isolated, withdrawn and are reluctant to leave the comfort of our home and surroundings. In late life it is not uncommon to make a new friendship with someone who shares interests, hobbies and views on life or who perhaps shared similar interests in their earlier life and is keen to reminisce on the 'good old days'.

> *Friendship is born at the moment when*
> *one person says to another:*
> *'What! You too? I thought I was the only one.'*
>
> **C.S. Lewis**

This experience can make both parties feel more connected, understood and supported, and provide an excellent opportunity to reminisce, share old memories and joint interests. Friendships can improve our outlook on life and reduce complications of poor health. There have been a number of new and close friendships, relationships and even marriages, established in late life across retirement villages and supported accommodation. Being open to meeting new people and being willing to step outside of the comfort zone where you may not know anyone, can profoundly influence the quality of your interactions and engagement.

Another elder once shared, 'It is hard to meet positive people around here,' referring to his home environment within residential care. This sentiment highlights the importance of attitude and perspective in forming new friendships. The concept of viewing the glass as half full or half empty comes to mind. In residential care settings, it can be challenging to find individuals who maintain a positive outlook, especially when faced with health issues and other life changes. However, adopting a positive attitude can make a significant difference in one's ability to connect with others. Focusing on the positive aspects of life, such as shared interests, common experiences and mutual support, can help foster meaningful connections. Encouraging a positive environment within residential aged care can also play a crucial role in helping residents form new friendships. Additionally, activities that promote social interaction, such as group outings, hobby clubs and communal dining, can create opportunities for residents to meet and bond with others.

In this chapter, we explored strategies for maintaining a positive attitude and creating an environment that supports the formation of new friendships. By focusing on the positive, we can help elders build strong, supportive relationships that enhance their overall wellbeing and reduce isolation and loneliness.

AFFIRMATIONS

Friendships provide a vital source of support, joy and connection, especially during times of emotional change and grief. Here are some helpful affirmations to support elders in the process:

1. I embrace the possibility of new friendships with an open heart.

2. I am not limiting myself and opportunities to make new friendships.

3. I feel safe with my friends and family.

4. My friends make me laugh, and that gives me joy.

5. My closest friends make the best company.

6. I trust that new connections will bring positive experiences into my life.

7. My friends and I encourage one another in all our efforts.

8. I welcome new friendships and the joy they bring.

9. I will make my friendships beautiful and fulfilling.

10. I love making friends that I genuinely admire.

Part IV

Boosting Physical Engagement

'I do as I feel, and I like to stay active and be around people. I still want to keep moving. If I sat down, I think I'd just give up,' says Toni Stahl, who still works out regularly at age 100!

It should come as little surprise that there is a strong connection between physical activity and physical engagement. The two interrelated terms are equally important throughout life, as they promote our overall health and wellbeing. We know that everyone should be active most days, and preferably every day. Unfortunately, the reality is far from it. Current global estimates suggest that one in four (25%) adults do not get enough physical activity (World Health Organization, 2023). It is predicted that our elder counterparts may, in fact, be even less active.

Let's explore why this may be the case. As we age, we may find it difficult to keep up with our hobbies and interests and need to make modifications in line with our physical tolerances. Looking at ways to modify what we do is more helpful than stopping activities altogether, which can lead to social isolation and withdrawal. Common themes that come up when discussing reduced physical engagement in late life include confidence, potential embarrassments and overall stresses and vulnerability.

In this section, we will review strategies that can boost physical engagement in late life through a range of face-to-face activities on an individual and group basis. We will cover approaches that are simple and adaptable, regardless of the elder's health status and environment. Being out of the comfort zone can be terrifying but is also the place where we build resilience, improve self-actualisation, develop a growth mindset and greater self-efficacy.

CHAPTER 10

The Power of Face-to-Face Connections

I don't think anything replaces the face-to-face meetings and the personal connections that you get when you're in the same room or same place with people.

Annamie Paul

Human connection is a deep bond formed between people when they feel seen, heard and valued. Such a powerful statement can be difficult to measure but can certainly be felt when we are physically close to our loved ones, as opposed to connected via phone, video link or reading an email. Our connections to friends, family members and even pets shape our identity and perception of who we are as individuals, provide us with a sense of fulfillment, and help minimise the risk of developing loneliness and isolation. How do those in-person connections change as we age? In this chapter, we will explore the importance of face-to-face connections, the common obstacles to maintaining them in late life, and strategies to overcome these challenges.

Face-to-face connections in late life offer numerous benefits. In-person interactions can help elders feel more connected, improve their physical health and build resilience. Human connection is most powerful in a face-to-face context, where we can read each other's body language and feel each other's physical presence, rather than guessing how someone feels. The fear of isolation and loneliness can feel deadly, and just knowing that there is someone else there can ease the burden. Loneliness can have a profound impact on our mental and physical health, leading to feelings of despair and hopelessness. For many elders, the absence of regular social interactions can exacerbate these feelings, making everyday life feel difficult and overwhelming. However, the simple knowledge that someone is there for them can provide immense comfort and relief.

Having a support system, whether it's a close friend, family member or even a neighbour, can make a significant difference. It reassures us that we are not alone in our struggles and that there is someone who cares about our wellbeing. This sense of connection can alleviate the weight of loneliness and provide a sense of security and belonging. Moreover, regular social interactions can help maintain cognitive function, improve mood and even boost the immune system. Engaging in meaningful conversations, sharing experiences and simply being present with others can create a positive ripple effect on our overall health and wellbeing. In essence, the presence of a supportive network can transform the experience of ageing, turning it from a period of isolation into one of connection and community.

The Power of Face-to-Face Connections

> **Did you know?**
> Up to 93% of communication is non-verbal. This highlights the importance of our body language and tone in how we communicate and convey information.

During genuine connections, people exchange positive energy and build trust. This type of interaction makes you feel heard and understood, gives you a sense of belonging, and boosts your confidence. There's a sigh of relief when you realise, 'Yes, you completely and truly understand how I feel.' The positive energy can be difficult to 'see', but it can certainly be felt between people, even if they do not necessarily exchange words and are just sitting side by side. So much of our communication is non-verbal and a lot can be said by someone's body language. Similarly, when we experience social pain – a snub, a cruel word or interaction – the feeling is as real as physical pain and can affect us for hours, days, months or years. Face-to-face connections can therefore enhance our wellbeing and impact it negatively if we are not experiencing a strong bond with another human being.

Evolving Connections

When our connections change through life, especially with shifts in roles and responsibilities, we may experience changes in our social circles, leading to new relationships and sometimes the loss of old ones. This can impact our sense of belonging and support network. There are many transitions that we experience throughout life, regardless of our marital status, career choices or whether we have children. We can transition from being a happily married couple to a caregiver and care recipient, or from a child-parent relationship to parenting an elderly parent. Regardless of our identity and role, the power of our connections and support network can help us navigate these life stages, providing support, encouragement and opportunities to reflect.

Our in-person connections can be significantly impacted by various factors. Changes in hearing can make it difficult to follow conversations, leading to misunderstandings and feelings of isolation. Similarly, changes in vision can affect our ability to read facial expressions and body language, which are crucial for effective communication. These challenges are often not easily overcome by aids and appliances. While many elders may be open to getting aids, using them regularly is another story. Certainly, there are a number of hearing aids, glasses, walking sticks and frames tucked away from sight and mind, destined to never see the light of day. It's almost as if they have joined the witness protection program for unused accessories!

Cognitive changes, such as memory loss or slower processing speeds, can also hinder our in-person interactions, making it challenging to keep up with conversations or remember details, particularly if they were not heard properly in the first place. Additionally, face masks and social distancing, while necessary for health and safety, can create physical barriers that obscure facial expressions and muffle speech, further complicating our ability to connect with others. These factors combined can make in-person interactions more challenging, but with awareness and adaptive strategies, we can still maintain meaningful connections.

Covid-19 Pandemic and Physical Engagement

In Chapter 6, we examined the social aspect of the pandemic on wellbeing. In this section, we will focus more on the impact of the pandemic on physical engagement. Since 2020, with the onset of the Covid-19 pandemic, we have become even more aware of the power of face-to-face connection and the impact of its absence on the quality of our lives.

Although the self-isolation experience has improved our computer skills and digital communication, nothing can replace the power of being connected with another human being and checking in with a loved one face-to-face. Many elders who may be socially isolated report missing connections with friends they can no longer visit, relatives who may be far away, or loved ones who have passed away. The grief, longing and loneliness can at times feel overwhelming.

At the same time, the fear of contracting a respiratory illness can be frightening. What if it sets back physical health? What if it causes complications? Additionally, the lack of face-to-face interactions may have delayed the detection of health changes in a loved one. Perhaps their cognitive changes have further advanced, or their mobility has reduced.

'I just want to see your face.'

These words were frequently spoken by residents in residential aged care when greeted by a staff member in full Personal Protective Equipment (PPE) or even with surgical masks. Many already had several health challenges and often the lack of visibility of worker faces and non-verbal body language made it more difficult to understand what was spoken and the tone in which it was delivered. For those impacted with dementia, the request to remove the mask was perhaps a bit sterner, as a colleague shared when an elder had said to her, 'take that muzzle off'. Our elders, along with the youngest members of our society, perhaps found it most difficult to accept the presence of masks and reduced face-to-face connections.

When we are discussing in-person interactions and particularly during the pandemic, it is evidently critical to keep elders safe and the face masks were in place to minimise the spread of the virus. However, at the same time they also highlighted the importance of our body language, effective communication, social interaction and strong connection with one another. Some strategies that assisted many who had to use face masks during outbreaks include writing down information, simplifying the message conveyed, using gestures and allowing additional time.

Sensory Impairment

Hearing and vision are the most commonly impacted senses in later life, affecting physical engagement. Hearing loss can be problematic for individuals and their families trying to communicate with them. It is not uncommon for older individuals to avoid using hearing aids, often finding them uncomfortable, inconvenient and unpleasant to see. This can result in frustration, misunderstandings and breakdowns in communication. It is important to communicate the impact of impaired communication on both parties and highlight the benefits of using hearing aids to protect relationships and maintain connections.

Physical Activity and Physical Engagement

Understanding the relationship between physical activity and physical engagement is essential. Although these concepts might seem intertwined like yin and yang, it is important to differentiate and measure them individually to promote better health outcomes for older adults.

Physical activity is often a nostalgic topic for older adults. Many reminisce about their past activities, such as playing tennis or golf, but struggle to identify what keeps them active in the present moment. Several factors contribute to this reduction in physical activity, including changes in health status, environment and support networks. Health setbacks, such as falls or balance issues, can significantly impact an elder's confidence and ability to move independently. This fear of becoming a burden often leads to reduced mobility, causing further physical deterioration and increased dependency on support.

According to the World Health Organization (2023), physical activity encompasses all movements, including structured exercise programs, sports, active recreation, play and walking. It can occur indoors or outdoors, be simple or complex, and be structured or unstructured. The term 'exercise' can be intimidating for older adults, especially those with previous health setbacks. However, avoiding movement can lead to more disconnection and physical decline. Identifying suitable activities and aids, such as those recommended by physiotherapists or occupational therapists, can help boost mobility and prevent or delay health problems. Regular physical activity strengthens muscles, enabling elders to maintain independence in their daily activities.

Physical engagement involves the social aspect of being active, focusing on interactions with others in the same environment. In recent years, online presence through social media and devices has increased, helping to boost elder engagement. However, physical engagement, both indoors and outdoors, is crucial for the physical and emotional wellbeing of older adults. Staying active through various activities can enhance safety, alertness, confidence and overall wellbeing. It can also reduce the risk of falls and physical setbacks.

Confidence plays a significant role in physical activity. Too much confidence can increase risks, while too little can result in missed opportunities for engagement and health maintenance. Recognising the right level of confidence in a person is essential for encouraging safe and beneficial physical activity.

To determine if a person has the appropriate level of confidence in their physical activities, consider these telling signs:

- **Observation:** Monitor their willingness to engage in activities without excessive fear or overconfidence.
- **Feedback:** Seek input from the individual and their caregivers about their comfort and confidence levels.
- **Assessment:** Use tools and assessments conducted by health professionals to evaluate their physical capabilities and confidence.

By understanding and addressing these aspects, we can encourage older adults to remain physically active and engaged, ultimately improving their quality of life.

In this chapter, we discussed the importance of human connection, especially face-to-face interactions, for older adults. These connections build trust, foster belonging, and enhance wellbeing through non-verbal communication. We examined how changing roles and responsibilities, like becoming a caregiver or care recipient, affect social circles and support networks. Maintaining in-person connections is vital but can be challenging due to sensory impairments like hearing and vision loss. The Covid-19 pandemic highlighted the emotional toll of isolation and the importance of physical engagement. While digital communication helped, the lack of face-to-face interactions underscored the need for clear and meaningful connections. Finally, we addressed the impact of sensory impairments on communication and the importance of using aids to maintain relationships. Promoting their use can help protect connections and improve the quality of life for older adults.

In essence, maintaining physical engagement and face-to-face connections is crucial for enhancing overall wellbeing and transforming the ageing experience into one of connection and community.

AFFIRMATIONS

In-person connections foster a sense of belonging and emotional support, which are essential for navigating life's changes and challenges. Here are some helpful affirmations to assist the process.

1. I am proud of myself.

2. I focus on what I can control.

3. Spending time with another person face-to-face brings me great joy.

4. I look for opportunities to connect with others.

5. I do not let setbacks affect my motivation and drive to connect with others.

6. A bad day does not mean a bad life.

7. Every day is an opportunity to spend time outdoors.

8. Nature gives me peace of mind.

10. My life is worth living.

11. No matter how trivial, I incorporate some type of physical activity into my daily life.

CHAPTER 11

One-on-One Wellbeing Activities

We are always the same age inside.

Gertrude Stein

One-to-one in-person activities play a crucial role in enhancing the wellbeing of older adults, particularly those in later life. These personalised interactions provide opportunities for meaningful connections, tailored support and individualised attention, significantly improving mental, emotional and physical health. Engaging in activities such as reminiscence therapy, gentle exercises or simply sharing a conversation can help alleviate feelings of loneliness and isolation, foster a sense of purpose and promote overall happiness. By focusing on the unique needs and preferences of each individual, one-to-one activities can create a supportive and nurturing environment that enhances the quality of life for older adults. In this chapter, we will explore various strategies to boost individual engagement, identify common barriers, and provide effective methods to overcome these obstacles.

Individual activities to boost physical engagement are usually easily identifiable but often unsustainable for long periods, especially for those living in residential care where staff may not have the time to provide continuous one-to-one support. As one wellbeing officer shared, 'Everyone wants individualised support, but I just cannot sustain that all day, every day.' However, it is not always necessary to be available for extended periods; the quality of engagement with leisure and wellbeing staff, nursing staff and volunteers is more important than the quantity. Sometimes, simple and brief strategies can be more powerful than prolonged conversations, particularly for older adults with sensory or cognitive impairments who may have difficulties hearing and sharing ideas or retaining attention for long periods. We need to keep in mind the 'quality over quantity' principle. It's not about the length of time spent but rather the meaningful and impactful interactions that make a difference. By focusing on the quality of engagement, we can ensure that even brief moments are enriching and fulfilling for the individuals we support.

Regardless of an individual's health status, the first step is to organise one-on-one catchups in comfortable environments. If the older adult lives in their own home, try meeting them outside or in the backyard. Spending time outside can be a calming experience, helping them become more aware of their surroundings and reducing the busyness of thoughts that may be going through their heads. If the older adult lives in residential care, take advantage of outdoor covered balcony areas, gardens or even the carpark to get some fresh air.

Listening Skills

One of the easiest and quickest ways to boost engagement with another person is to listen. Listening is a skill essential for empathy, compassion and open communication. Spending just 5 minutes with someone, actively listening, can boost their confidence, self-esteem and brighten their day.

We have two ears and one mouth so that we can listen twice as much as we speak.
Epictetus

To become a better listener, give your full attention to the speaker by eliminating distractions and focusing on the conversation. Show your engagement through body language, such as nodding, maintaining eye contact, and using facial expressions that reflect understanding and interest. Avoid interrupting and let the speaker finish their thoughts, demonstrating respect and allowing them to express themselves fully. Ask open-ended questions to encourage deeper sharing and use reflective statements like, 'What I hear you saying is ...' to ensure accurate understanding. Empathise with the speaker by acknowledging their emotions and validating their experiences. Provide thoughtful and constructive feedback when appropriate, and be patient, giving the person time to articulate their thoughts without rushing or finishing their sentences. By integrating these steps into your interactions, you can enhance your listening skills and build stronger, more meaningful connections.

Easy Strategies to Boost Individual Activities

Looking for ways to boost individual engagement with older adults? Here are some friendly and engaging ideas that can be implemented regardless of where they live. For additional insights from various professionals on enhancing individual wellbeing, check out the archived podcast 'The Voice of Aged Care' at www.wisecare.com.au/podcast.

- **Gardening and cooking/baking:** These activities can be therapeutic, providing a sense of accomplishment and fostering social interaction.

- **Storytelling sessions, mindfulness and meditation:** These practices can alleviate stress and improve mental wellbeing.

- **Board games, puzzles and technology workshops:** Stimulate cognitive function while having fun.

- **Dance and movement classes, book clubs and intergenerational activities:** Enjoy physical health benefits, engagement and connection with younger generations.

By incorporating these activities, we can foster a supportive and engaging environment that enhances the quality of life for older adults in both residential care and community settings.

Addressing Physical Isolation in Later Life

Addressing physical isolation in later life is crucial, as interactions through daily activities and support extend beyond mere physical assistance. If you work in aged care settings, you might be the only person the elder engages with on a given day. One of our roles is to be a 'bringer of hope,' restoring hope in those who have lost it. By developing skills and improved ways of coping and adjusting, a person can view their world and the outside world with more gratitude, hope and wisdom.

To support elders who are physically isolated and reluctant to engage in activities or services, start small by initiating brief interactions and actively listening. Encourage small wins, such as suggesting a 5-minute walk or sitting outside in the sunshine. Provide reassurance to alleviate fears about venturing outside. In aged care homes, consistently encourage attendance in the dining room for social, physical and emotional benefits. In a home environment, encourage sitting at the front or back of the property, and in retirement living, consider participating in on-site activities. Through these strategies, we can help physically isolated elders feel more connected, supported, and hopeful.

> The longer the person is isolated,
> the harder it will be to re-engage.
>
> At all times try to minimise prolonged isolation with simple strategies and steps that the person can complete and gain a sense of accomplishment.

Addressing Physical Barriers in One-on-One Interactions

Avoiding stimuli that predict danger is essential for survival. However, maladaptive avoidance, where individuals overestimate threats and avoid both safe and dangerous situations, can be detrimental to wellbeing. This blurred distinction between danger and safety can lead to excessive avoidance, a core feature of anxiety disorders, PTSD and OCD. Such avoidance prevents individuals from confronting maladaptive threat beliefs, maintaining disordered anxiety and high levels of psychosocial impairment.

Strategies to Address Physical Barriers in One-on-One Interactions

- **Provide reassurance:** Offer comfort and gradual exposure to new activities, ensuring physical support and the use of recommended aids.

- **Ensure companionship:** If the person needs to walk with someone, make sure a companion is available.

- **Consult professionals:** Review the situation with a physiotherapist if necessary.

- **Normalise activities:** Incorporate outdoor activities into the daily routine, such as having lunch in the courtyard or taking a walk in the garden after meals.

- **Encourage brief outdoor time:** Assure the older person that spending a few minutes in the sunshine will not make them too hot, cold or wet. The benefits of outdoor exposure outweigh the risks.

- **Utilise nature's calming effect:** Help the person analyse the visual space from top to bottom. Observe the sky (stars, sun, moon, clouds), the horizon (trees, buildings, animals), and the ground (flowers, insects, raindrops). This can be a calming and grounding experience.

Addressing the Emotional Barriers

One of the main barriers to spending time with others and being outdoors is the perception that leaving the comfort of one's home is dangerous. This conclusion can arise from physical health changes, mobility issues, difficulty navigating uneven grounds and the busyness of the world, where crowded environments and the need for mobility aids can be daunting. Being out of the comfort zone can be overwhelmingly frightening and frustrating, leading older adults to fear being outdoors, feel anxious and stressed, and retreat indoors. This cycle can be difficult to break, as the fear of going outside and the frustration of feeling stuck at home reinforce each other.

The fight-or-flight response is an automatic physiological reaction to an event perceived as stressful or frightening, regardless of whether the actual threat is real. The perception of threat activates the sympathetic nervous system and triggers an acute stress response that prepares the body to fight or flee. Physical signs of the fight-or-flight response include dilated pupils, pale or flushed skin, rapid heart rate and breathing, and trembling. In times of danger, our bodies become more aware of the surroundings, with dilated pupils allowing more light to enter the eyes for better vision. Blood flow to the surface areas of the body is reduced, while flow to the muscles, brain, legs and arms is increased. Heartbeat and respiration rate increase to provide the body with the energy and oxygen needed to fuel a rapid response to danger. Muscles tense and become primed for action, which can cause trembling or shaking. While there is a psychological explanation for these symptoms, the emotional threat also needs to be processed.

In recent years, we have learned more about how our brain works and perceives threats. We have learned about the role of the amygdala in processing emotions and how it affects our stress response rate when overwhelmed. A new term, 'amygdala hijack' refers to when strong emotions 'take over' the thinking part of the brain. Emotions like anger, fear or extreme excitement can make it more difficult to regulate our stress response and return the body to a calm state.

So, how do we learn to respond instead? Keep up the regular practice of getting outside more frequently; the more often we do it, the less likely we are to perceive the activity as stressful. Take small steps to gradually incorporate getting outdoors into your daily routine. Listening to gentle music, focusing on breathing and practising mindfulness strategies can also help to promote a sense of calm. No music player? No problem – play a song on your phone, TV or radio. Easy classical music can be sourced from various places; don't overthink it.

Activity – Addressing Fears

Sometimes we may feel unqualified and uncomfortable addressing the fears that older adults have about their daily activities. This uncertainty can stem from not knowing them well enough or being unsure if they are genuinely uninterested in the task or simply worried and in need of gentle encouragement. Over time, you will be able to discern which category their behaviour falls into and, with practice, get to know the person and their preferences.

However, addressing these fears can be straightforward with simple strategies. It is important to understand what is going on for the individual, what contributes to their fears, and to assess the situation to determine the level of fear they are experiencing. When discussing fear, we need to clarify whether it is a 10 out of 10 fear, like being chased by a lion in the Serengeti, or a 1 out of 10 fear, like removing a dead insect from the floor. Understanding the level of fear an elder may experience is crucial. The following scale can be helpful in the process.

Fear Scale

| 0 Not at all Frightening | 5 Moderately Frightening | 10 Most Frightening |

Here is an example:

Question: Hello Dawn, how do you feel about going for a short 5-minute walk with me to check out the rose bush? What score would you say it would be from 0 to 10 for you today?

Dawn's response may be:

0-5	go ahead
5-10	do not go ahead unless Dawn insists that she wants to go and see the rose bush; stick with activities that only evoke 0-5 fear scale score, then progress gradually to more difficult tasks

Keep up 0-5 regularly to build confidence and self-esteem. The more often it is completed, the better Dawn will feel about her skills and ability to engage with her physical environment.

Tackling Engagement Issues: Practical Solutions

Let's delve deeper into what constitutes a problem and how we can assist an elder if they report an issue with one-on-one engagement. Understanding the specific nature of the problem is crucial, as it allows us to tailor our support effectively. By identifying the root causes and contributing factors, we can develop targeted strategies to help the elder overcome these challenges and enhance their engagement. You do not necessarily need to be a counsellor to work through this with someone; however, if a person has additional support needs, be sure to escalate your concerns.

A practical approach to problem-solving involves working through the problem statement, as outlined below. The formula focuses on articulating the trigger (i.e. when the event occurs), the behaviour that follows (what happens), the consequences (because I think/fear that), and finally, the impact (which affects). Using this formula, we can create an example common for elders, such as:

Trigger: When I am asked to join group activities in the common area.

Behaviour: I feel anxious and refuse to participate.

Consequences: Because I think/fear that I will be judged by others or that I won't be able to keep up with the activities.

Impact: It affects my social interactions and leads to feelings of loneliness and isolation.

Problem statement

WHEN (trigger)

WHAT (behaviour)

BECAUSE I THINK / FEAR THAT (consequences)

WHICH AFFECTS (impacts)

To assess the impact of a problem, you can rate it on a scale from 0 to 6, where 0 means it is not a problem, 2 indicates a moderate problem, 4 signifies a severe problem, and 6 represents a very severe problem. Consider the impact on day-to-day life by asking, 'What impact does the problem have on daily activities?'

Incorporating Mindfulness in One-on-One Interactions

Nature has varied benefits for different people, but being in the open air is universally beneficial. Exposure to sunlight can improve mood and recovery, while introducing plants indoors can bring a sense of calm. Spending quiet time outdoors can be very grounding, and encouraging participation in exercise programs and activities can help maintain physical health. It's important to be mindful of fall risks in both aged care and home settings and to take steps to minimise these risks. Encouraging regular movement, such as walking to the toilet or taking short strolls, can prevent prolonged sitting and promote overall wellbeing.

Grounding Exercises

'Getting Grounded in Nature' involves exercises to bring oneself into the present moment. These can be quick strategies like taking three deep 'belly breaths' or longer exercises like meditation. Here is a short grounding activity to practise a few times a day:

1. *Five things you can see:* Acknowledge five things you can see around you, such as clouds, trees, flowers, leaves or birds.
2. *Four things you can touch:* Acknowledge four things you can touch, such as your hair, a bench, or the ground under your feet.
3. *Three things you can hear:* Acknowledge three things you can hear, whether external sounds or internal ones like your belly rumbling.
4. *Two things you can smell:* Acknowledge two things you can smell, such as flowers, fresh air or rain.
5. *One thing you can taste:* Acknowledge one thing you can taste, like coffee, a biscuit or a sandwich from lunch.

One-to-one in-person activities are fundamental to enhancing the wellbeing of older adults. These personalised interactions not only provide meaningful connections but also offer tailored support and individualised attention, significantly improving mental, emotional and physical health. By addressing the unique needs and preferences of each individual, we can create a supportive and nurturing environment that fosters a sense of purpose and promotes overall happiness.

Throughout this chapter, we have explored various strategies to boost individual engagement and identified common barriers such as physical and emotional challenges. We discussed practical methods to overcome these obstacles, including listening skills, easy strategies for boosting individual activities and techniques to address fears. By implementing these strategies, we can effectively reduce feelings of loneliness and isolation, enhance the quality of life for older adults, and ensure that they receive the compassionate care they deserve. Let's continue to focus on creating an inclusive and supportive environment where older adults can thrive and maintain their dignity and wellbeing.

AFFIRMATIONS

Forming individual connections can provide valuable social support, reduce feelings of isolation and enhance overall wellbeing. Here are some helpful affirmations to support elders in the process:

1. I cherish the meaningful connections I have with others.

2. Each conversation I have brings me closer to understanding and empathy.

3. My relationships are built on trust, respect and mutual care.

4. I find joy in sharing moments with those I care about.

5. I am open to forming new, meaningful connections.

6. I listen with compassion and speak with kindness.

7. Every interaction is an opportunity to strengthen my bonds with others.

8. I value the unique qualities each person brings into my life.

9. I nurture my relationships with love and understanding.

10. My connections with others enrich my life and bring me happiness.

CHAPTER 12

Group Wellbeing Activities

Getting old is like climbing a mountain; you get a little out of breath, but the view is much better!

Ingrid Bergman

Imagine for a moment that your entire life has been turned upside down by a series of unwelcome changes affecting your health, support network, environment or sensory system. This exercise may be challenging, as our minds are accustomed to interpreting situations from our current perspective and often struggle to process hypothetical scenarios and potential emotional responses. It is difficult to fully grasp what we would think and feel if the life we once knew no longer existed.

Being alone or with others may seem like a simple task today, but if we too experienced such unwelcome changes, our habits might shift dramatically. For some older adults, impacted by numerous changes in late life, the idea of joining a group can be petrifying, filled with uncertainty, fear and a sense of overwhelm. Their confidence may have diminished after a fall; a musical may no longer be enjoyable due to hearing loss and the adjustment to hearing aids; or going to the movies may not feel the same without their spouse.

In this chapter, we will explore how to encourage and facilitate group activities for elders who have experienced unwelcome changes in late life, whether they are living in their own homes, in retirement living settings or in residential care. By doing so, they can learn new strategies to engage with their environment, reduce the impact of loneliness and isolation, and build confidence and resilience. Through compassionate support and understanding, we can help them navigate these challenges and foster a sense of belonging and wellbeing.

Addressing the Barriers to Physical Engagement

Staying in the comfort of one's own home brings a sense of calmness, peace and joy amidst the busyness of today's world. During the Covid-19 pandemic, we learned the importance of staying at home to minimise the risk of contracting and spreading the virus. The home environment provides a sense of safety, security and comfort. For many, activities at home create a sense of fulfilment – cooking, gardening, crafting, reading and watching movies.

However, when our ability to complete these tasks is impacted, staying at home can lead to feelings of disconnection, loneliness and fear, which may result in social isolation. An elder with declining mobility once reflected, 'Staying indoors daily will eventually make you sick.' This perspective highlights the importance of recognising the physical and emotional factors that contribute to social disconnection.

Addressing the barriers to social and physical engagement in late life is crucial. Whether older adults are living in their own homes, retirement living settings or residential care, creating opportunities for engagement can help improve their quality of life. By understanding and addressing these barriers, we can foster a supportive environment that encourages meaningful interactions and reduces the impact of isolation.

Understanding and Tackling Isolation Barriers for Older Adults

The first step is to identify the barriers to engagement, which will help us understand how to address the issue.

	Barriers	Suggestions
1.	Memory changes	Mindfulness activities one-on-one or in a group setting, reminiscence, memory games (sudoku, crosswords, find-a-word, puzzles). Adjust complexity level accordingly.
2.	Sensory issue	Addressing each sensory impairment separately (e.g. hearing loss and low vision) and support the use of aids and appliances on a regular basis.
3.	Confidence	Support to pick up a new easy to master hobby, regular activities to boost engagement and mobility.
4.	Lack of social connections	Support to make new friendships, spending time outdoors watching people walk past, creating small opportunities for engagement.

	Barriers	Suggestions
5.	Grief and loss	Listening ear and connecting to more support, if deemed appropriate.
6.	Poor mental health	Escalating concerns to GPs. Connecting with free and confidential services (See Appendix for more details).
7.	Loneliness	Creating opportunities for connection through facilitated events, volunteers and buddy programs.
8.	Mobility issues	Escalating concerns to GP. Connecting with exercise physiologist, physiotherapist, occupational therapist. Supporting attendance at structured exercise program.

Group Engagement

Group time offers numerous benefits, such as being with peers, sharing experiences and making new connections. However, facilitators often encounter several challenges when running groups. They may struggle to find the time to plan and run group sessions amidst their other responsibilities or feel uncertain about how to begin organising and facilitating group activities. Some facilitators might feel unqualified, lacking the necessary skills or qualifications to effectively lead group sessions. Additionally, keeping participants engaged and motivated can be challenging, especially if the group is diverse in terms of interests and abilities.

Managing group dynamics, such as ensuring everyone has a chance to speak and resolving conflicts, can also be difficult. Resource constraints, including limited materials and space, and privacy concerns when discussing sensitive topics, further complicate the process. Despite these challenges, the benefits of group time for both participants and facilitators are significant. Whether older adults are living in their own homes, retirement living settings or residential care, running groups is beneficial. Providing opportunities for elders to connect with others who share similar experiences can foster connections, shared experiences and friendships.

How to achieve a successful group

Creating a successful group involves several key steps that ensure smooth planning and execution.

Step 1: Source a facilitator. This is a crucial step, as the group cannot run without a facilitator. Facilitators can come from various backgrounds, such as carers, lifestyle personnel, allied health professionals, chaplains or volunteers.

Step 2: Find suitable participants. Identify up to 20 individuals interested in connecting with others and sharing their experiences and learnings. Participants should come from diverse backgrounds and abilities but share a common interest and goal.

Step 3: Content and group rules. Decide on the topics to be covered, group rules and privacy guidelines. Determine what will be shared, how and by whom, as well as the frequency and duration of the meetings.

Step 4: Review success and feedback. Establish how the group's success will be measured, how feedback will be collected and how achievements will be celebrated.

Step 5: Sustainability. Determine how the program will be sustainable in the long term.

Wellness Groups

Many providers offer wellness group programs for older adults. These groups provide a supportive environment where older adults can connect with others, share their experiences and develop new skills to enhance their quality of life. Often facilitated by mental health professionals, wellness groups focus on specific goals such as reminiscence, social skill building, fostering a sense of community and supporting adjustment to health changes.

Wellness groups offer numerous benefits, including:

- **Enhanced social connections:** Participants often form new friendships and support networks, which can significantly improve their emotional wellbeing.

- **Improved coping skills:** Through group discussions and activities, participants learn new coping strategies to manage stress and adapt to changes in their lives.

- **Increased confidence:** Engaging in group activities and sharing experiences can boost participants' confidence and self-esteem.

- **Better mental health:** Regular participation in wellness groups has been shown to reduce symptoms of depression and anxiety among older adults.

Whether older adults are living in their own homes, in a retirement village or residential aged care, wellness groups play a crucial role in enhancing their quality of life by providing opportunities for meaningful connections, personal growth and emotional support.

Wellness Adventure

The Wellness Adventure Program was designed in 2011, to reduce isolation and build confidence and new skills in elders facing late-life changes. Recognising a gap in preventative group interventions, I launched the program in various aged care homes in Sydney. It quickly gained popularity by helping elders connect, form friendships and improve coping skills. The program was later introduced in retirement villages, where it also met the emotional and social needs of elders.

This award-winning program boosted resilience and enhanced wellbeing in elders at risk of mental health conditions. It was a weekly group program, running for 8 weeks with up to 16 participants. Topics included reminiscence, coping strategies, problem-solving, psychoeducation on self-care and memory improvement. The program eventually expanded to retirement villages and residential care settings across Australia. Feedback was overwhelmingly positive, with participants reporting a 50% decrease in their perceived risk of developing depression after completing the program during the Covid-19 pandemic (April–June 2021).

Here's some feedback from facilitators:

Facility Manager (Adelaide): *'We have received such amazing feedback regarding this training and the ongoing rollout.'*

Lifestyle Coordinator (Newcastle): *'I am so excited to be part of this project and to see the changes in my residents – they enjoy getting out of their rooms and our sessions. It has been transformational.'*

Lifestyle Coordinator (Sydney): *'We held our first class this week and WOW, what a response. I feel like I gained as much or more than my beautiful residents. The communication between the residents opened up so many pathways. I'm truly blessed to be a part of something so beautiful.'*

Chaplain (Mid North Coast NSW): *'I enjoy delivering the sessions with my colleague and working together to support our residents. It is fun!'*

And here's some comments from participants:

'I liked it very much. We got to know each other better. It was different from being in the dining room. I recommend this group to others.

'It's good to be around others. I like being in a group; it helps to spread the whole discussion.'

'I don't normally like groups, but I enjoyed it. The subject matter was interesting. I say to others it's worth giving it a go.'

'I thought it was very good and very helpful. I enjoyed being in a small group. I liked the information in the folder. I enjoyed the teaching and working and interacting as a group. I look forward to the group each week.'

'I really enjoyed it. It's good for me to live in the moment because I've always lived in the past. I enjoyed being in a small group. Yes, I'd recommend the group.'

'I liked all the interactions in the small group. I liked meeting new people. I enjoyed sharing my life and my opinions on the topics. I had a lot of things I could go back on to share with others. The last day of the group was the best because everyone talked.'

'I thoroughly enjoyed it. I'm new here. I saw into people, it was very interesting. My wife, she's a lot better because of the group. I've been independent for a long time, then came here. I enjoyed being in a small group.'

Group Wellbeing Activities

> As of late 2024, the Wellness Adventure Program is on hold as we focus on other projects and priorities. However, it will be re-offered in the future. Previously, the program was available for licensing to other organisations, allowing them to use Wise Care's intellectual property under a 12-month agreement. This included facilitator training and all course materials. If you are interested, please reach out for more details.

In this chapter, we explored the significance of group activities in enhancing overall engagement. Group activities offer numerous benefits, such as fostering social connections, promoting physical interaction, and providing opportunities for individuals to connect and share experiences. In the post-pandemic era, the value of physical connection has become increasingly evident, benefiting everyone, including older adults. Group programs, such as exercise groups, discussion groups and recreational activities, help combat isolation, improve mental health and enhance overall wellbeing by encouraging regular physical activity and social interaction.

Wellness groups, in particular, play a crucial role in fostering emotional and social connections, as well as promoting physical interaction among participants. These specialised programs focus on specific goals, such as reminiscence, social skill building and supporting adjustment to health changes. By participating in wellness groups, older adults can build support networks, develop new skills and enjoy a sense of community and belonging.

AFFIRMATIONS

Joining groups can be challenging, especially when one is facing multiple health issues. However, these connections can provide valuable social support, reduce feelings of isolation, and enhance overall wellbeing. Here are some helpful affirmations to support elders in the process:

1. Shared experiences allow me to learn more about myself and others.

2. I am not too old to make a new friend.

3. New learnings allow me to make positive changes in my life.

4. I love learning and embracing all that comes my way.

5. Spending some time alone is okay; a lot is NOT.

6. I am connected to earth and mother nature.

7. I make powerful connections with others.

8. I choose to make positive changes to my health and wellbeing.

9. Looking after myself and my health is my priority.

10. I still matter, have a voice that needs to be heard, and memories to be made.

Afterword

Reflecting on the journey of writing this book, I am filled with a deep sense of gratitude and accomplishment. This has been a transformative experience, not only in terms of research and writing but also in personal growth and understanding of all the pieces of the puzzle needed to support an older person experiencing unexpected changes in late life.

I want to extend my heartfelt thanks to everyone who supported me along the way: my research colleagues, clinicians, community and residential care workforce, and older people and their families. Your support has been invaluable, and I am deeply grateful.

My mission was to translate research and evidence-based strategies into practical steps that could be easily incorporated into daily activities. I hope this book serves as a useful resource for those working in aged care and those caring for older people living in their own homes or in residential care settings.

Since completing this book, there have been new developments in how we work in aged care in Australia. The New Aged Care Act 2024 includes the Support at Home Program, set to launch in July 2025. Enhanced quality standards now require providers to adhere to stricter quality standards and a robust regulatory framework. Additionally, there are stricter controls around aged care advice to prevent financial harm from unqualified advice. All these changes will have a profound impact on how we support elders and ensure their dignity and respect is maintained.

I am excited to share that the advice in my book will help with these recent changes in the industry. I encourage readers to stay informed and engaged with these ongoing discussions.

As you close this book, I urge you to reflect on the ideas presented and consider how they apply to your own life and work. Navigating changes in aged care can be challenging, and I am here to support you. Remember, every small step towards improvement is a step worth celebrating. Let this be a starting point for further exploration and action.

Looking ahead, I am excited about focusing on building and maintaining worker wellbeing and resilience.

You can reach me at julie@wisecare.com.au or follow my updates on Instagram (https://instagram.com/drjuliebajic) or Facebook (https://facebook.com/drjuliebajic).

Thank you for being a part of this journey. May we continue to learn, grow and inspire one another.

Today and always,

Julie Bajic Smith

APPENDIX

Helpful Contacts

Australia

There are several important service provider numbers to know:

- **Aged Care Grief and Bereavement Support:** The Australian Centre for Grief and Bereavement (ACGB) offers support for aged care residents, home care recipients, their families, friends, community workers, residential aged care staff and external organisations associated with aged care. Contact Grief Australia at 1800 22 22 00 or email covidagedcare@grief.org.au.
- **Beyond Blue:** Beyond Blue provides support for mental health and wellbeing. They offer a range of services including counselling, resources and community forums. Reach them at 1300 22 4636 or visit their website for more information.
- **Lifeline:** For immediate support, Lifeline is available at 13 11 14. Did you know that every 30 seconds, a person in

Australia reaches out to Lifeline for help? They offer 24/7 crisis support and suicide prevention services.

- **Suicide Call Back Service:** Provides 24/7 phone and online counselling for people affected by suicide. This service is available at 1300 659 467. They offer free, professional support for those struggling with suicidal thoughts, as well as people supporting someone at risk.
- **Survivors of Suicide Bereavement Support:** This service provides specialised support for people who have lost someone to suicide. Contact them at 1300 767 022 for compassionate support and resources to help navigate the grief and healing process.
- **Swinburne University – Wellbeing Clinic for Older Adults:** Operating for over a decade, this not-for-profit counselling and support service for the residential aged care community offers support via phone or video calls. Their counsellors are provisionally registered psychologists, social work interns and counselling postgraduates, supervised by experienced practitioners. Contact them at +61 3 9214 3371 or email wellbeingclinic_agedcare@swinburne.edu.au.

New Zealand

- **Lifeline:** 0800 543 354 (0800 LIFELINE) or free text 4357 (HELP)
- **Samaritans:** 0800 726 666
- **Suicide Crisis Helpline:** 0508 828 865 (0508 TAUTOKO)
- **Healthline:** 0800 611 116

United States

- **988 Suicide & Crisis Lifeline:** Dial 988 for immediate support for suicidal thoughts or emotional distress.
- **SAMHSA National Helpline:** 1-800-662-HELP (4357) for information and referrals for mental health and substance use issues.

Helpful Contacts

- **National Domestic Violence Hotline:** 1-800-799-SAFE (7233) or text 'LOVEIS' to 22522 for confidential assistance.
- **Crisis Text Line:** Text 741741 for free, 24/7 support from a trained crisis counsellor.
- **Disaster Distress Helpline:** 1-800-985-5990 for mental health issues after a disaster.

United Kingdom
- **Samaritans:** Call 116 123 for 24/7 support or email jo@samaritans.org
- **Shout Crisis Text Line:** Text 'SHOUT' to 85258 for confidential 24/7 support.
- **Mind Support Line:** Call 0300 102 1234 for mental health support.
- **SANEline:** Call 0300 304 7000 for out-of-hours mental health support.
- **National Suicide Prevention Helpline UK:** Call 0800 689 5652 for support with suicidal thoughts (6pm to midnight every day).

Extra Affirmations

Here are some additional affirmations to consider incorporating into your own daily routine and to share with older adults. These positive statements can help boost self-esteem, foster self-love and encourage a positive mindset. Repeat them regularly to reinforce these empowering beliefs.

- ❖ I am enough.
- ❖ I am working on me, for me.
- ❖ I am going to be okay.
- ❖ Good things are coming to me.
- ❖ I am stronger than my problems.
- ❖ The past is over.
- ❖ I am my own priority.
- ❖ I love myself.
- ❖ I deserve endless love and happiness.
- ❖ My body deserves to be loved.
- ❖ I am proud of myself.
- ❖ I believe in me.
- ❖ I am destined for success.
- ❖ I am enough, I did enough, I can let go.
- ❖ I am letting go of doubt and fear.
- ❖ It's okay to not be okay, but I can get support.

- ❖ I can only change myself.
- ❖ My life is worth living.
- ❖ I am worthy of my own love.
- ❖ I focus on what I can control.

These affirmations can serve as a powerful tool to enhance your mental and emotional wellbeing.

Reference List

Attig, T. (2001). Relearning the world: Making and finding meanings. In R. A. Neimeyer (Ed.), Meaning reconstruction & the experience of loss (pp. 33–53). *American Psychological Association.* https://doi.org/10.1037/10397-002

Brydon, A., Bhar, S., Doyle, C., Batchelor, F., Lovelock, H., Almond, H., Mitchell, L., Nedeljkovic, M., Savvas, S., & Wuthrich, V. (2022). National survey on the impact of COVID-19 on the mental health of Australian residential aged care residents and staff. *Clinical Gerontologist*, 45(1), 58-70. https://doi.org/10.1080/07317115.2021.1985671

Centers for Disease Control and Prevention. 'Mental Health Basics'. *Centers for Disease Control and Prevention*, 2013. Web. 22 Apr. 2016.

Cohen, C., & Sokolovsky, J. (1989). *Old men of the Bowery: Strategies for survival among the homeless.* New York: Guilford Press.

Crane, M., & Warnes, A. M. (2002). Resettling older homeless people: A longitudinal study of outcomes. Sheffield: *Sheffield Institute for Studies on Ageing*, University of Sheffield.

Fiske, A., & Arbore, P. (2001). Future directions in late life suicide prevention. *Omega: Journal of Death and Dying*, 42(1), 37–53. https://doi.org/10.2190/3T4G-T5U2-Q724-E0K8

Garofalo, D. (2013) The whats and whys of social networking for academic libraries, *Building Communities*, Chandos Publishing, 1-25, https://doi.org/10.1016/B978-1-84334-735-4.50001-4.

George L.K., Ferraro K.F., Carr D., Wilmoth J.M., & Wolf D.A. (2015) *Handbook of Aging and the Social Sciences: Eighth Edition*, 1-531.

Grenier, A., & Sussman, T. (2022). '5: Poverty and late-life homelessness'. *Critical Gerontology for Social Workers*. Bristol, UK: Policy Press. Retrieved Jun 23, 2024, from https://doi.org/10.51952/9781447360476.ch005

Grimby A. 'Bereavement among elderly people: Grief reactions, post bereavement hallucinations and quality of life'. *Acta Psychiatrica Scandinavica* 1993;87(1):72–80.

Hafemeister, T. L. (2003). Financial abuse of the elderly in domestic settings. In R. J. Bonnie & R. B. Wallace (Eds.), Elder mistreatment: Abuse, neglect, and exploitation in an aging America (pp. 13). Washington, DC: National Academies Press (US). Available from: https://www.ncbi.nlm.nih.gov/books/NBK98784/

Holwerda, T. J., Deeg, D. J. H., Beekman, A. T. F., van Tilberg, T.G., Stek, M.L,. Jonker, C,. & Schoevers, R.A. (2014). Feelings of loneliness, but not social isolation, predict dementia onset: Results from the Amsterdam Study of the Elderly (AMSTEL). *Journal of Neurology, Neurosurgery & Psychiatry*, 85(2), 135-142.

House, J.S., Landis, K.R., & Umberson, D. (1988) Social Relationships and Health, *Science* 29 Jul 1988, 241, 4865, pp. 540-545 DOI: 10.1126/science.3399889

Klass, D., Silverman, P. R., & Nickman, S. L. (Eds.). (1996). *Continuing bonds: New understandings of grief*. Taylor & Francis.

Kübler-Ross, E. (1997). *On Death and Dying*. United States: Scribner.

Makhado, G., Ntuli, B., Zungu, L., Thovhogi, N., Mphekgwana, P. M., Sogolo, L. L., & Modjadji, P. (2024). The Wellbeing of Healthcare Workers During COVID-19 Era in Public Primary Health Facilities in Johannesburg, South Africa. *International Journal of Environmental Research and Public Health*, 21(3), 372. doi:https://doi.org/10.3390/ijerph21030372

Reference List

Mayo Clinic. (2021, January 4). *Complicated grief: Symptoms and causes*. Mayo Clinic. Retrieved from https://www.mayoclinic.org/diseases-conditions/complicated-grief/symptoms-causes/syc-20360374

Miller, M. (2012). 'Complicated Grief in Late Life', *Dialogues in Clinical Neuroscience*, 14, 2.

Nair, S. P., Quigley, A. L., Moa, A., Abrar, A. C., & Chandini, R. M. (2023). Monitoring the burden of COVID-19 and impact of hospital transfer policies on australian aged-care residents in residential aged-care facilities in 2020. *BMC Geriatrics*, 23, 1-11. doi:https://doi.org/10.1186/s12877-023-04154-z

National Institute on Aging. (2024, October 5). *Goal B: Behavioral and psychological factors*. National Institute on Aging. Retrieved from https://www.nia.nih.gov/about/aging-strategic-directions-research/goal-behavioral-psychological-factors

Perissinotto, C. M., Stijacic Cenzer, I., & Covinsky, K. E. (2012). Loneliness in older persons: A predictor of functional decline and death. *Archives of Internal Medicine*, 172(14), 1078-1083. https://doi.org/10.1001/archinternmed.2012.1993

Petersen, M. & Parsell, C. (2014). Homeless for the First Time in Later Life: An Australian Study. *Housing Studies*. 30. 1-24. 10.1080/02673037.2014.963522.

Royal Australian College of General Practitioners. (2021, January 4). Mental health. In Silver Book: Part A. Retrieved from https://www.racgp.org.au/clinical-resources/clinical-guidelines/key-racgp-guidelines/view-all-racgp-guidelines/silver-book/part-a/mental-health#ref-num-11

Rumi, J. (2004). *Rumi: Selected Poems* (C. Barks, J. Moyne, A. J. Arberry, & R. Nicholson, Trans.). Penguin Books. Retrieved from https://www.scottishpoetrylibrary.org.uk/poem/guest-house

Stroebe, M., & Schut, H. (1999). The dual process model of coping with bereavement: Rationale and description. *Death Studies*, 23(3), 197–224. https://doi.org/10.1080/074811899201046

Tierney, L., Doherty, K., & Elliott, K. (2022). Distressed, detached, devalued and determined: Aged care workers' experiences of the COVID-19 pandemic. *Australian Journal of Advanced Nursing* (Online), 39(3), 45-53. doi:https://doi.org/10.37464/2020.393.661

Weber, Z. (2001). *Good Grief – How to recover from grief, loss or a broken heart.* Margaret Gee: Sydney.

White, J., Falcioni, D., Barker. R., Bajic-Smith, J., Krishnan, C., Mansfield, E., & Hullick, C. (2024). Understanding Dementia Carer Experiences Before Admission to a Residential Aged Care Facility: Implications for Integrated Care. *Journal of Applied Gerontology*. 2024 Jul 18:7334648241261454. doi: 10.1177/07334648241261454. Epub ahead of print. PMID: 39023911.

White, J., Falcioni, D., Barker, R., Bajic-Smith, J., Krishnan, C., Mansfield, E., & Hullick, C. (2024). Persisting gaps in dementia carer wellbeing and education: A qualitative exploration of dementia carer experiences. *Journal of Clinical Nursing*, 00, 1–13.

Wilson, D. (1995). *'We will need to take you in': The experience of homelessness in old age.* Edinburgh: Scottish Council for Single Homeless.

Wolitzky-Taylor, K., Castriotta, N., Lenze, E., Stanley, M., & Craske, M., (2010). Anxiety disorders in older adults: A comprehensive review. *Depress Anxiety* 2010;27(2):190–211

Wordel, J.W. (2009). *Grief counselling and grief therapy: a handbook for the mental health practitioner 4th ed.* Springer Publishing Company.

World Health Organization. (2020). *Risk reduction of cognitive decline and dementia: WHO guidelines.* Retrieved February 12, 2023, from https://www.who.int/publications/i/item/risk-reduction-of-cognitive-decline-and-dementia

About the Author

Dr. Julie Bajic Smith is a compassionate and dedicated registered psychologist with over 15 years of clinical experience in aged care. As a board-approved psychology supervisor, she provides invaluable clinical supervision to intern psychologists and other mental health professionals. Julie is also a respected researcher and writer. Her doctorate research focused on the wellbeing of home care workers, and her postdoctoral research explored supported decision-making in dementia.

Julie's recent publications highlight the emotional challenges faced by carers when moving a loved one into residential care, as well as the stress and burnout experienced by the aged care workforce. She has extensive experience in assessing and applying psychological treatments to older adults. Her first book, *Beyond the Reluctant Move*, focused on enhancing emotional wellbeing in residential aged care environment.

Julie has also developed several preventative psychological group programs for older adults entering residential care, which have been recognised with Positive Living in Aged Care Awards in Australia. Her work continues to make a significant impact on the lives of older adults and their carers, offering support, understanding and practical solutions during challenging times.

Work With Me

Julie is available for organisational consultation, training and support to enhance worker resilience in supporting older adults. Working in aged care today comes with its own unique challenges. Clients often have diverse and complex needs, and teamwork might not be as robust as it once was. Balancing busy work and personal lives can feel overwhelming, leaving little time for self-care.

For more information about how Julie can assist your organisation, please visit wisecare.com.au.

Notes

www.ingramcontent.com/pod-product-compliance
Lightning Source LLC
Chambersburg PA
CBHW020411080526
44584CB00014B/1282